Quiet Your Mind

Mindfulness Meditation Practices to Reduce Stress, Manage Anxiety and Worry, Improve Mental Health, and Create Inner Peace

Steven Schuster

stevenschusterbooks@gmail.com

Copyright © 2018 Steven Schuster. All rights reserved.

No part of this publication may be reproduced, stored in a retrieval system, or transmitted in any form or by any means, electronic, mechanical, photocopying, recording, scanning or otherwise, except as permitted under Section 107 or 108 of the 1976 United States Copyright Act, without the prior written permission of the author.

Limit of Liability/ Disclaimer of Warranty: The author makes no representations or warranties with respect to the accuracy or completeness of the contents of this work and specifically disclaims all warranties, including without limitation warranties of fitness for a particular purpose. No warranty may be created or extended by sales or promotional materials. The advice and recipes contained herein may not be suitable for everyone. This work is sold with the understanding that the author is not engaged in rendering medical, legal or other professional advice or services. If professional assistance is required, the services of a competent professional person should be sought. The author shall not be liable for damages arising herefrom. The fact that an individual, organization of website is referred to in this work as a citation and/or potential source of further information does not mean that the author endorses the information the individual, organization to website may provide or recommendations they/it may make. Further, readers should be aware that Internet websites listed in this work might have changed or disappeared between when this work was written and when it is read.

For general information on the products and services or to obtain technical support, please contact the author.

Table of Contents

Chapter 1: What is Mindfulness?.................................9

Chapter 2: Proprioception, Interoception, and Mindfulness..23

Chapter 3: Mindfulness Based Stress Reduction.....35

Chapter 4: The Mind-Changing Magic of Meditation 57

Chapter 5: Acceptance and Commitment Therapy ..75

Chapter 6: Wu Wei - The Do-Nothing Principle.....87

Chapter 7: Energy Management With Mindfulness 99

Chapter 8: Mindfulness in Relationships and Work 117

Final Words...133

Reference 135

Endnotes 145

Chapter 1: What is Mindfulness?

Have you ever walked into a room and looked around in confusion, wondering why you were in there? Have you ever driven your car and arrived at your destination without remembering how you got there? Or when you checked your watch, did you have to look at it again because you forgot the time? What about if you were asked to share how you spent the first hour of your day? Would you be able to remember it in detail? If not, you are not alone. All of us have been in those very situations more often than we would probably like to admit.

If you, like so many of us, find that you can't remember parts of your day, it doesn't necessarily signal a memory problem. It may just mean that you aren't truly present in your head.

Why did you get this book? Perhaps you'd like to be more aware of your everyday life and thoughts. Maybe you wish to reduce stress in your life. Or you'd like to harness some health benefits to enjoy a more restful sleep. Even though they sound simple, everyday problems, for many of us, overcoming these issues represent a great challenge because we are exposed to more stress and feel more anxiety than ever before. We feel pressure on a daily basis to succeed, to increase the palette of our achievements, and become self-critical even self-judgmental when we don't. We run through our days, trying to catch up with our expectations, and end up falling in the bed exhausted after such a hectic day.

All we can think of are the weekends that would hopefully ease our minds. But when the long-awaited weekend arrives, we can't stop ruminating on the things we didn't achieve the past days or getting prematurely anxious about what the next week will bring. This is an unsustainable living condition if we wish to stay healthy in the long term.

The overwhelming living conditions we experience today has motivated many people to turn to practicing mindfulness. This practice helps us to wake up, be aware of the present moment so we can experience life with our five senses. Mindfulness helps us with many other life-improving things like how to communicate in a patient, calm manner, and how to recognize our unhealthy habits. We also become kinder, more tolerant, and less judgmental with ourselves.

What is Mindfulness?

We become in a mindful state when our mind is completely focused on the present moment and attentive to what is happening right now while gently acknowledging and accepting our feelings, thoughts, and bodily sensations.

"Mindfulness is the basic human ability to be fully present, aware of where we are and what we're doing, and not overly reactive or overwhelmed by what's going on around us." - Mindful.org

Focusing our mind for any extended period of time is not something that comes easily and naturally to most of us. The mind wanders more often than we might be aware. The majority of the time, our mind drifts into places of negative thoughts which can cause us to feel stress, anxiety, regret, shame, and unhappiness. Did you know that eighty percent of the average person's daily thoughts are negative? [i] Having these negative thoughts as they form an unconscious mental chatter can leave us with a feeling that life is hard, and the struggles we have to go through aren't worth it.

I experienced this in my own life when my wife was in the hospital with a very serious health condition. When I was visiting her, my mind would wander to all the things I should be doing and was neglecting at work and at home. When I was teaching, my mind was in the hospital. Whenever I wasn't at home, I would feel stressed, anxious, and guilty about what I should be doing there to be a good father to my children. No matter where I was, I was never completely present.

This period of my life triggered the irreversible desire in me to become more mindful, take meditation more seriously, and live each of my days with my loved ones as if it would be the last. It was not until I experienced the agony of a three-month-long fear of losing my wife that I actually started to feel the weight of the benefits of these practices. It seems like a cliché, but the fear of loss and pain can teach us the greatest lessons.

Mindfulness is something everyone can practice and benefit from. It is a way of life. Mindfulness brings awareness and focus to everything we do, and it helps to cut down on needless stress by eliminating the negative thoughts that creep into our minds. Every second that we spend in mindfulness improves our lives.

You don't have to only rely on your personal experiences (or mine) to know that this is true.

Science backs it up as well. Mindfulness benefits our health, happiness, work, and relationships. When we are in a mindful state we are more innovative, effective, resilient, and are better problem-solvers.

The best—or easiest—way to practice mindfulness is through meditation. I will talk in detail about meditation practices in the next chapters. For now, I'd like to prove to you that there are scientifically proven, life-quality-enhancing benefits of practicing mindfulness.

The Scientific Benefits of Mindfulness

Researchers are becoming more interested in the practice of mindfulness as studies continue to prove its many benefits. Currently research is being conducted to study how the brain responds to mindfulness, how relationships benefit, and how physical and mental health can improve when mindfulness is actively practiced. The following extracts are just a sampling of the studies being conducted to discover how mindfulness enhances our well-being.

- **Improves the Brain and the Immune System**

A study published in *NeuroReport* in 2005 found that people who meditated long-term showed thicker cortical regions in their brains related to attention and sensory processing than those who did not practice meditation. The findings went on to suggest that practicing mindfulness through meditation might offset the cortical thinning that naturally occurs as people age.[ii] This study is not alone in concluding that the practice of meditation, and thus achieving mindfulness, may affect the structure and neural patterns present in the brain. Scientists are now seeing the results extend beyond the meditation sessions and into the daily lives of those who regularly meditate.

A study conducted in 2003 investigated how an eight-week training course on how to practice mindfulness through meditation would impact the brains and immune systems of the participants. It found evidence that an area of the brain connected to positive effect showed increased activation, and that the immune systems were able to produce more antibodies after the participants went through the meditation training.[iii]

Another recent study followed Chinese undergraduates who underwent five days of meditation training for twenty minutes a day. It found that when presented with a stressful laboratory task, the students who were trained in how to meditate showed a faster decrease in levels of the stress hormone cortisol, which indicated that they were better able to regulate stress than a group of students who had received relaxation training. The undergraduates who learned to meditate also reported feeling less anxiety, depression, and anger than their counterparts.[iv]

- **Mindfulness Meditation Improves Relationships**

There is evidence showing that mindfulness training can improve the quality of a person's relationships. A University of North Carolina at Chapel Hill study found correlation between practicing mindfulness and enhanced relationship quality. The couples participating in the study reported a greater feeling of closeness, increased acceptance of each other, and an overall improvement in general satisfaction with their relationships. A study in 2007 drew a similar conclusion. It showed a connection between the improved quality of communication of couples and the practice of mindfulness.[v]

Practicing mindfulness also benefits familial relationships. Parents of children with developmental disabilities indicated that their mindfulness training resulted in their increased satisfaction with their parenting skills, interacting socially more often with their children, and experiencing less parental stress. The same researchers conducted a study in 2006 investigating parents of children with autism and the same results, demonstrating an increased satisfaction with their parenting skills and relationships, applied. Both studies showed that the children benefited from their parents practicing mindfulness, as the children themselves showed a decrease in aggressive and noncompliant behavior.[vi]

- **Mindfulness Improves Fields of Education**

Studies are now being conducted to see if having children practice mindfulness in an educational setting may prove beneficial. A study followed children in grades one to three who went through a twelve-week program of breath awareness and yoga, which was delivered fortnightly. The findings showed that the students who went through the program showed an increase in attentiveness, improvements in social skills, and a decrease in test anxiety when compared to students who did not have the training.[vii]

UCLA's Mindful Awareness Research Center

conducted two pilot studies that followed preschool and elementary students who went through an eight-week mindful awareness practices training program for two thirty-minute sessions each week. Their findings showed improvements in self-regulatory abilities of the children who went through the training when compared to students who did not receive training. These studies show that practicing mindfulness in a school setting can have benefits for students.[viii]

- **Other Benefits of Mindfulness**

In a 2013 Massachusetts General Hospital Study, researchers found that mindfulness can reduce anxiety. They followed ninety-three people with a diagnosis of generalized anxiety disorder who underwent a mindfulness-based stress reduction group intervention for eight weeks. These participants showed a marked drop in their anxiety levels, which was much greater than the people who simply went through stress management education.[ix]

Mindfulness meditation was found to reduce age and

race bias in a 2015 Central Michigan study. The participants were given either a mindfulness or a control audio to listen to. Those who listened to the mindfulness audio showed a drop in their implicit age and race bias as opposed to the group who did not. The professor who led this study revisited it again later, asking the participants to play a trust game where they were asked to look at pictures of people from different races and identify who they would trust to help them win money and who they would expect to steal money. The people in the mindfulness group trusted people from both racial groups almost equally, while those in the control group selected the white people in the pictures as trustworthy more often than the black people.[x]

A study conducted by researchers Ellen R. Albertson, Kristin D. Neff, and Karen E. Dill-Shackleford found that mindfulness can increase body satisfaction in women. In their study, those who underwent a three-week self-compassion meditation training showed more gains in self-compassion and body appreciation and a reduction in body shame and the feelings that their self-worth should be based on their appearance compared to the group who did not. These effects were found to still be present even three months later.[xi]

A 2010 study published in the *Consciousness and Cognition Journal* found that cognitive abilities can be improved after even a short period of mindfulness training. Half of the participants in the study went through four days of mindfulness training while half of them listened to an audio book during the same time. Those who went through the mindfulness training reported less anxiety and fatigue and showed a more marked improvement in their visual-spatial processing skills and memory than those who did not.[xii]

These reports are just a fraction of the accumulating proof on why mindfulness and meditation are good for you. But neither will be actually helpful if I'm talking about studies and benefits, right? You came here to have some hands-on practice. Let's get started!

Chapter 2: Proprioception, Interoception, and Mindfulness

Ask an eight-year-old what the human senses are, and they'll generally give you five: taste, smell, sight, sound, and touch. These are the ways humans and many animals experience the physical world, or so we're taught. The true definition of sense is much more complicated.

What do you hear right now? The clack of typing on a keyboard? The sound of a truck rushing by? Sirens? The ocean? What would you do if you heard a mouse rustling in your garbage? You'd probably jump, and your heart would start to race, right? What do you smell? What are you sitting on? What do you see? All this information is important to navigating everyday life and helps keep us alive and safe. But it's not the only information our body physically processes.

Do you like to take hot showers? How do you know if they're hot or cold? You could say this comes from touch, but your body isn't just processing whether it's coming into contact with water. It's also processing whether the temperature of that water feels good or is dangerous. This is called thermoception, and it's also a very important sense. It allows you to determine whether the environment you're in is a healthy temperature for your body. Think about how long you've been reading this chapter. You know whether it's been a short time or a long time, and you'd probably even be able to guess it to the minute. Your body generally knows what "twenty minutes" and "two hours" feels like, and this perception of time passing is also a sense.

Stand with your hands at your sides. Now close your eyes and touch your nose with your index finger. Open your eyes, look at the ceiling or sky, put your hands at your sides, and touch your chin with your thumb. You didn't have to make much of an effort to do that, did you? Now try to put on lipstick or eyeliner without looking in a mirror. It's a much harder task! Why is this?

Your body used a sense called proprioception when you touched your face. This sense helps you know where your body parts are in space, relative to your body and other objects, which means that it's best at detecting where your body parts are in relation to your body. This is why it's so hard to do makeup without a mirror—there's an extra implement involved! You can kick a soccer ball or serve in a tennis game because of proprioception! You might think of it as "hand-eye coordination," but it's much more elaborate. It allows you to perform the smallest physical tasks, like picking up an object, without thinking about how to do each motion. Neurons send signals to the brain that orient the body in relation to its environment, thus helping us sense where we are in the world. This makes it a very important sense!

Have you ever woken up with a cold and felt dizzy and unable to smell or taste anything? This is because of how all our senses are wired together. Taste and smell are especially closely connected, which is why a lot of food tastes bland when our noses are stuffy. The tongue has taste buds that detect five flavor groups: salty, sweet, sour, bitter, and umami. The first four are commonly known; you can test them out by putting chips, then chocolate, then a lemon wedge, then coffee on your tongue. Umami is a little harder to define, but it's the savory flavor that you find prominently in cheeses. Other sensations, like spice, mint, and alcohol burn are related to other nerve reactions and not your taste buds. There are thousands of taste buds on the tongue, and they have short life cycles, which is why tongue burns from hot chocolate or pizza, for example, disappear after a few days.

Your nose can also distinguish between thousands of odors and can inform your taste experience, which is why smell is so important for enjoying food. Neurons are triggered by specific odors, which then send a message of what they are to the brain. The human nose is much less sophisticated than animal noses; that's why dogs are so effective at search-and-rescue operations! As we age, our noses and taste buds also lose sensitivity. This is why adults often find spicy foods, alcohol, and other "acquired tastes" more pleasurable than children do.

Touch and proprioception are also closely related and part of the same sensory grouping in the brain, which deals with pressure, body position, and pain. The skin is the most helpful indicator for touch, because its neurons react to pressure, temperature, and pain sensations. You know this if you've ever accidentally touched a hot stove. Every other touch sensation, such as softness or roughness, is a combination of these three basic groups.

The dizzy, out-of-it feeling you get when you have a cold comes from an imbalance in the fluid inside your ears. This is called the vestibular system and is similar to proprioception because it helps your body orient itself. A blockage due to sinus congestion or infection messes that system up and confuses your brain, which causes that congested feeling.

Interoception

Proprioception is the most well-documented additional sense in scientific literature, but there are two other senses that are closely related. They are called exteroception and interoception, and if proprioception is in the middle of a scale of perception, they are the two extremes. Exteroception is perceiving what's going on in our environment (jumping at mouse noises, seeing how people react to us), while interoception is perceiving what's going on within ourselves.[xiii] Interoception can be as simple as noticing indigestion, or feeling that your feet are sore after a long shift at work. However, it can also mean being mindful of your breathing in and out while doing yoga or practicing breathing exercises or mantras to combat panic attacks. Practicing deliberate interoception is something we often do in modern life without realizing the scientific term, especially when participating in mindfulness or wellness exercises.[xiv]

In a study published in the journal *Frontiers of Human Neuroscience*, a team from Ulm University in Germany found that interoception provided positive benefits for participants. The interoceptive exercises undertaken were meditation and another mindfulness exercise. In the first study, the non-control group did an audio-guided body scan exercise for eight weeks, while the control listened to an audiobook. In the second study, the team compared the body scan group with a control group that did no audio exercise whatsoever. Participants were evaluated based on a heartbeat perception task and a confidence rating for that task, along with assessment on a scale of "interoceptive awareness." The researchers found that in the first group, the body scan exercise improved performance on the perception task, although it didn't affect the other outcomes tested. In the second study, the researchers found the same result. This means that these interoceptive-improvement mindfulness exercises helped people become more aware of their own heartbeats, and by extension their own bodies.[xv]

All this is important because improved interoceptive accuracy might improve overall health, although the scientific community is still unsure if this is true according to the authors of the study. This is important, because this study and others seems to validate the claim that mindfulness and therapeutic exercises that focus on interoception can improve quality of life for people with conditions like clinical anxiety, PTSD, eating disorders, and obesity.

Proprioception, Interoception, and Mindfulness

Proprioception and interoception-focused training can be beneficial for our physical health as well as our mental health. One of the biggest dangers for the elderly is falling, which can cause serious injury and even death. Falling becomes more common as humans age because proprioception gradually becomes weaker over time as ability to perform physical activity decreases. Thus, the elderly often experience decreasing physical coordination and find it harder to perform everyday tasks.[xvi]

We depend on proprioception to be able to walk through a dark room without losing our balance and falling, to keep our eyes on the road as we drive while pressing the pedals with our feet, and to perform other quotidian tasks. We often don't think about these sorts of necessary activities; movements like breathing, hearts beating, and walking are largely unconscious for typically-abled people. However, when these movements become difficult and proprioception decreases, many daily tasks become dangerous. Taking the stairs could be lethal. A run in the park could end in a sprained ankle. A few steps across a dark room to turn on a light could result in a concussion.

Mindfulness exercises, yoga, and other proprioception and interoception-centric activities can help strengthen the body's proprioceptive abilities. Being able to trust one's body is a wonderful thing, and highly-developed proprioception and interoception can grant people the physical and mental freedom to do all the things they want to do, even as they lose mobility into old age. Getting to know your own body ultimately keeps you safe and allows you to navigate the world with more confidence.

There are several exercises you can do at home to improve proprioception and interoception. Here is one that requires no outside equipment, workout clothing, or excessive physical effort:
First, sit up straight with your feet fully touching the ground, either in a chair or on the floor. Put your hands where they feel comfortable and can rest.

Then, notice your breath. You don't have to make it deep or make noise, just pay attention to when you inhale and exhale, and what comes in between.

Next, focus on one sense at a time, for about a minute (use your perception of time!). You don't have to notice them in any particular order, just make sure you give each one attention.

- Hearing: Focus on sounds you're hearing around you. Don't judge them or react to them. They are simply around you. You could hear your stomach gurgle, or your breath, or noise from the street below. Notice how far away from you they are. You might hear subtle sounds you wouldn't have heard otherwise. Enjoy them and realize they are now perceived because you are focusing on them.
- Smell: Close your eyes and notice the smells in your environment. There could be many different ones, depending where you are and what is happening there. Try to identify as many as you can.
- Sight: Look at your environment and notice the shapes, colors, and textures of things. Try to notice things you wouldn't otherwise have seen.

- Taste: Pay attention to the taste of your mouth. Is there the aftertaste of food? If there is food, what are the flavors? What do your tongue, saliva, teeth, cheeks, and breath feel like? Notice their taste.
- Touch: Notice the feel of your clothes on your body, and your body's contact with where you're seated. What is the pressure on your feet like? Is the floor cool or warm? Can you feel any textures? Pick up an object and notice how it feels if you need more focus.[xvii]

After you go through all five senses, how does your body feel? Has it changed from when you began the exercise? Noticing these details can help with your interoception and proprioception, and center you if you are noticing things like anxiety, lack of coordination, or soreness in your body.

Chapter 3: Mindfulness Based Stress Reduction

Mindfulness Based Stress Reduction (MBSR) was developed in the 1970s at the University of Massachusetts Medical Center by Professor Jon Kabat-Zinn. In 1979, he went on to open the Mindfulness Stress Based Reduction Clinic at the University of Massachusetts Medical Center. MBSR uses yoga, body awareness, and mindfulness meditation in the hopes of helping people to become more mindful.

Kabat-Zinn described mindfulness as "moment-to-moment non-judgmental awareness." The goal of the MBSR program is to help us stop dwelling on the past and stop worrying too much about the future by teaching us how to focus on the present. It is believed that by giving our attention to the environment around us and how we react to it, we will be better equipped to cope with the challenges we face.

Mindfulness Based Stress Reduction seeks to help people with pain and other physical and mental conditions which may at some point best be treated outside of the hospital setting. It strives to help people relax and reduce their stress to show improvements in their overall quality of life. Over the years, MBSR has grown in popularity so much that it is now practiced in hospitals around the world. Nearly eighty percent of medical schools today offer some form of mindfulness training to their students. MBSR is now considered a form of complementary medicine and is often utilized in the field of oncology.[xviii]

Does it Work?

Mindfulness Based Stress Reduction has been used to help treat people with a variety of health concerns such as chronic pain, eating disorders, mood disorder, anxiety disorder, ADHD, substance abuse disorder, depression in expectant mothers, and insomnia across all age groups and backgrounds. It can also be helpful to people who are having difficulty accepting and coping with the fact that they have a serious medical condition.

Scans of the brain have found that gray matter density changed in areas of the brain that involve regulating our emotions and learning and memory processing after practicing MBSR. Studies have also found an improvement in immune system functioning correlating to the practicing of MBSR. Practicing mindfulness meditation has proved helpful in reducing feelings of depression among expectant mothers and improving the bond they report feeling with their unborn children. This reduction in depression was also reported among people who suffered from chronic illness.[xix]

Researchers studied the response to pain in people who participated in MBSR compared to people who did not participate in the mindfulness meditation. Brain scans revealed that the brains of both groups indicated they noticed the pain equally, but the participants of MBSR didn't transfer it into a perceived pain signal, so they registered a feeling of pain forty to fifty percent less often than the group who did not participate.

There are also more studies being conducted on the effectiveness of MBSR on other health concerns, but while the results are encouraging, they are too preliminary at this time to be conclusive.

There seems to be a small window of time when we can choose how we will react to the stress and pain we experience. If we are in the present, focused, and aware, we have a much better chance of choosing to respond in a more positive way. Thankfully, mindfulness gives us the ability to interrupt our autopilot habits and negative cycles that we would not have if we were unaware of what is happening in the present moment.[xx]

Some of the Most Popular MBSR Exercises and Techniques

There are many different ways to practice mindfulness. Here, I will highlight a few of the most popular methods. The type of mindfulness you are trying to practice will help you to determine the technique that would best suit your needs.

Simple Breathing Exercise

One of the most basic, yet amazing, mindfulness meditation techniques is breathing. It helps us become present by focusing on our rate of inhalation and exhalation.

How to practice Breathing Meditation?
Find a quiet place where nobody would disturb you for ten minutes. Sit down comfortably on a chair or pillow. Straighten your back to allow your breath to flow smoothly. Close your eyes. Let your shoulders loose and rest your arms gently in your lap.
Breathe in. Feel as the cold air enters your nostrils.

Trace the inhale as it goes through your body, filling your lungs. Then gently acknowledge that swift moment, that pause when your inhale turns into an exhale. Count one. Then slowly let the warm air out of your lungs, through your nostrils or mouth. Feel how the temperature of your breath changed. Take notice of the little pause when your exhale turns into an inhale. Count two.

Practice this breathing exercise for three, five, or ten minutes a day.

Focus Mindfulness

Since focus is the emphasis of this practice, the goal is to look inward and be attentive to what is going on in your mind. You need to get laser-focused on one experience. In order to maintain this intense focus, breathing is most often the method of choice for keeping yourself grounded.

One of the best aids of productivity is the ability to focus, to narrow down our attention onto something. By focusing we keep our eyes on our target. This is the key element of efficiency and concentration.

Unfortunately, our attention is limited and often gets diminished by distractions around us. How often do you find yourself distracted by social media, a chatty coworker, the need for a snack? More things compete to capture our attention than ever. Anchoring our attention has become a real challenge these days.

Focus Mindfulness helps improving one's focus by:

- drawing awareness on habits,

- deepening concentration skills,

- resisting distractions,

- learning to prioritize,

- and prevent informational and emotional overwhelm.

By learning to recognize your habits related to distractions, you'll become aware of them sooner and thus, overcome them in a timely manner and return your focus to your priorities. Noticing when you drift away is the first step for coming back.

How to practice Focus Mindfulness?

Find a quiet place where nobody will disturb you for ten minutes. Sit down comfortably on a chair or pillow. Straighten your back. Imagine that an invisible string is attached to your skull and keeps you in a straight position.

Close your eyes. Let your shoulders and arms rest gently. Take a few deep breaths. Inhale while counting to four. Notice the pause when your inhale turns into an exhale. Then gently let the air out of your lungs... two, three, four. Inhale again... two, three, four. Notice the pause. Exhale... two, three, four. Feel how the cool air enters your nostril at the beginning of the inhale and how warm air leaves your body as you exhale. With each breath you take, let go of just a bit more stress and tension. Relax your eyes, your jaw. Release any tension in your body. Whenever distractions arise, like thoughts, loud noises on the street, gently, let them go. Don't get caught in them. Bring your attention back to the breath.

Repeat this breathing exercise for about ten minutes.

Awareness Mindfulness

This mindfulness practice focuses on the external

more than the internal. It also focuses on the mind, but more as if you are a neutral observer looking in from the outside without passing any judgment. To practice this type of mindfulness, you begin by focusing on your breath. Then you attempt to look upon your thoughts, moods, and feelings as if they are separate from you and just passing by. You then choose one thought or emotion to focus on and quiet all of the others into the background. Finally, you let go of the one you focused on and just leave it behind.[xxi]

Another way to practice Awareness Mindfulness is to use sounds as a reminder to bring you back to the present moment. We use various devices to remind us of something. For example, we use alarm clocks to signal our wake-up time, we use birthday reminders, water drinking reminders, notebooks to pen in our schedule for the next week. Using a bell during mindfulness meditation is a gentle yet effective way to bring our minds back from wandering. The bell "wakes us up" to the present moment.

How to practice Awareness Mindfulness?

Find a quiet place where nobody will disturb you. Set your phone to one-minute timer sessions to make a sound, preferably a bell, at the end of each minute. You can also use a YouTube video, specific for this purpose.

Here is one– https://www.youtube.com/watch?v=kQrDC41LpkU– but you can find many others. The purpose of this practice is that each time you hear the bell, bring your attention back to your breath–in case it drifted.

Sit down comfortably on a chair or pillow. Pay attention to your posture. Keep your back straight. Allow the breath to flow easily. Relax your eyes, your jaw. Let your chest and abdomen be soft. Close your eyes. Let your shoulders and arms rest gently.

Take a few deep breaths to calm your body. Inhale Exhale. Pay attention to the point wherever you feel the breath the strongest. Follow your breath cycle from the beginning, to the middle, to the end. Let the breath enter and leave freely, without forcing it. Just follow its natural rhythm. Your breath becomes deeper as your mind and body relax. Whenever distractions arise, like thoughts, loud noises on the street, gently, let them go. Don't get caught in them. Bring your attention back to the breath. Continue breathing in and out.

Repeat this breathing exercise for about ten minutes.

In our daily lives there are many external triggers we can use as mindfulness reminders. Try to come up with three such triggers you could use to remind yourself to come back to the present moment during the day. This could be the ring of your office phone, the wall clock's sound, the bell of the elevator... Choose a sound of your liking and use it as a mindfulness reminder. Take a few breaths whenever you hear your trigger.

Body Scan

The body scan is a popular mindfulness technique.

How to practice Body Scan?

Lie flat on your back in a relaxed position. Let your legs part naturally. Keep your arms next to your body. Close your eyes and tune into your mind by following your breath. Breathe in, relax your body. Breathe out, let tension go. Take a few deep breaths, slowly expanding your lungs. Notice how it feels to be full of life-giving oxygen. Slowly exhale.

While keeping tuned in with the breath, shift your focus to your body. Start scanning your body at your toes or the top of your head and move your awareness all through your body, focusing on one area at a time. I will present a bottom-up version of Body Scan.

Breathe in to your feet and toes. Observe what you feel; is it tickling, numbness, pain, tension, or nothing at all. Whatever you feel is okay. Don't try to change what you feel. Simply accept the feeling, acknowledge it, and move on to your legs. Feel the full length of your legs and observe what you feel there. Scan your ankles and knees, calves and shins, your upper leg. If you come across an area that feels tight or sore, focus your breath and concentration on that area until it relaxes, and then move onto the next area. Move to your hips and pelvis, your abdomen and lower back. Breathe in to each of them, observing your feelings there. Then scan your chest and upper back, arms and legs. Finally, breathe in your shoulders and neck. Relax your face and scalp as you scan them.

Object Meditation
Object meditation is a technique where you choose an object that has special meaning to you or that you think is interesting to focus on.

How to practice Object Meditation?
Find a quiet place where nobody will disturb you for ten minutes. Sit down comfortably on a chair or pillow. Straighten your back. Imagine that an

invisible string is attached to your skull and keeps you in a straight position.

Direct the attention of all your senses onto the object and receive the information that your senses send to your brain about the object, including its size, shape, weight, texture, sound, taste, and smell. Let's say this object is your plush bunny. First, take a look at it as it is. Wander your eyes on its size, shape, colors, and details from the biggest to the smallest ones–like a tiny piece of filling sticking out through the stitches. Then take it into your hands–run your fingers through its texture, cuddle it, squish it to feel how soft it is. Notice how the toy gradually warms up in your hand. Open your ears, hear how it sounds when you squeeze this piece of personal memory. Can you hear the plush sizzling? Sniff it and try to identify familiar smells the toy captured during its faithful service. Gently observe this object for about ten minutes being fully present.

About the taste... Some objects can't be tasted. To

indulge your taste buds, there is another type of mindfulness meditation practice, mindful eating.

Mindful Eating

Mindful eating is a technique very similar to object meditation, except your focus is now on a food as you eat it slowly and notice everything about it.

How to practice Mindful Eating?

Sit down to your dining table with a piece of food. If this will be your first time to practice mindful eating, choose something small such as a piece of cherry, strawberry, or candy. Find a comfortable sitting position where your back is supported and tall. Relax your face, your neck and shoulders and take a few, deep breaths. Inhale, and fully exhale. Stretch your spine while you inhale and gently drop your shoulders at the exhale. Begin to notice the rising and falling sensations of your breath. Tune in to the present moment with the help of your breathing.

When you feel fully relaxed, take a moment to think

about your relationship with food. Do you overindulge often? Do you feel stressed when you eat too much or too little? Many people try to repress their stress, cure their anxiety, ease their pain with eating. But just like many other distractions, eating is not the solution for these issues. Trying to use food as a painkiller may give a short-term gratification but will leave a much more bitter taste in your mouth after you finish eating. Are guilt, shame, and embarrassment crawling into your mind after such occasions? If you have felt any of these negative emotions after eating, you are not alone.

The problem usually isn't with the food itself but rather with our attitude towards it. We can improve this relationship through mindfulness. Trying to eat in a purposeful, nonjudgmental way, only when we are hungry and consuming just as much as we need can significantly increase our self-esteem and decrease our weight. We can get rid of unhealthy eating habits.

When we eat mindfully, we are fully engaged in the process of eating. We pay attention to the texture, aroma, flavor, smells, and sounds. We recognize how full we are before, during, and after eating. Thus, chances to overeat are lowered. Eat slowly, fully taste each bite, emerge in the experience. It's also an important aspect to leave self-judgment and criticism off the table. Instead, we embrace our entire being with compassion and love. We nurture our body, the shell of our existence, and take care of it by not overeating.

Now bring your attention to your food. Let's say you have a piece of cherry. Before you eat it, take time to engage your vision in the eating experience. Look at the cherry, notice its full, healthy redness. It's almost bursting with sweet juice. Then take it into your hand, feel its smooth, sun-kissed skin. Bring it to your nose and smell its inviting aroma. Gently bring it to your lips and take a bite from it. Hear how the ripe fruit crunches between your teeth. Before you swallow it, take a moment to discover everything your cherry has to offer with your tongue. Observe its texture, its taste, its flesh. Allow a few moments with the taste in your mouth, then swallow it.

After you finish eating your cherry–or any other food you consume–don't forget to say thank you for the food you just had. Gratitude is a powerful feeling that liberates us from anxiety, the pain of scarcity and unfulfillment.

Walking Meditation
Walking Meditation is a technique that involves you taking a stroll at a relaxed, gentle, and familiar pace. It's a great way to practice mindfulness. When we walk mindfully, we notice things that we would fail observing otherwise. Sounds and smells are sharper, colors are more intense. We only need to pay attention.

How to practice Walking Meditation?
Start walking. Focus your attention on your lower body. Notice on how the different parts of your legs

feel as you walk and the way that your body moves. Feel how your foot leaves the ground, how your heels part and reconnect with the ground. See how each step feels. Do you walk lightly or do your steps feel heavy? What's your pace? Fast or slow? Pay attention on every detail of your steps. Notice how your weight moves with your steps, how your arms swing, how your entire body is involved in the simple process of walking. Try to make your breathing match your steps. How does your chest work together with your breathing?

When you have observed your internal feelings, widen your observation to your surroundings. Look with curiosity and amazement to the trees around you, the passing cars, the people walking on the street. Tune in all of your senses. Is it windy outside, sunny, or rainy? Now notice every sound around you. Are these sounds loud or quiet? Sharp or numb? What smells can you notice? Emerge into a full sensory experience.

Worry or Urge "Surfing"

With this technique you think of your thoughts as waves of water you are "surfing" on.

How to practice Urge "Surfing"?

Go to a quiet place where nobody will disturb you for ten minutes. Sit down comfortably on a chair or pillow. Straighten your back. Imagine that an invisible string is attached to your skull and keeps you in a straight position.[xxii]

Direct your awareness toward the negative thoughts and feelings that might be popping into your mind (if any). Imagine those negative thoughts as a wave that gets bigger and bigger until it reaches you. Then visualize yourself successfully riding the wave and watching the negative feelings continue to move away with the wave once it passes you by. This allows you to let go of the negativity instead of dwelling on it.

All of the practices presented above are from MBSR.

I believe in the power of the guiding principles of MBSR to impact the mind in a positive way. I do not want to encourage or deter anyone from trying these techniques or even Kabat-Zinn's eight-week mindfulness course, I am not tied by any personal or monetary interest in recommending it. I sincerely believe that whether to take the course is a personal decision that should be made by each individual after assessing his or her own risks and responsibilities. If, after giving it some thought, you decide that you want to try to practice mindfulness even by participating in a mindfulness course, there are opportunities available to you.

You could begin by conducting a simple internet search for MBSR teachers near you who received their certification from the Center for Mindfulness. There are also some online courses offered. The Sounds True website offers a MBSR course online that follows the same method as the Center for Mindfulness and the teachings of Jon Kabat-Zinn. Another online course is offered by Palouse

Mindfulness from a MBSR-certified instructor who trained at the University of Massachusetts Medical School. This course is based on the teachings of Kabat-Zinn, but it is not an exact copy of his work. These are just a few of the course offerings that are available. Many more can be found.

You can also try some online mindfulness meditation apps like Calm, or Headspace. These apps contain guided meditation practices narrated by professionals to celebrities.

Mindfulness Based Stress Reduction is a program that has had proven success in helping people with a variety of health concerns. There are many benefits that everyone can experience from it, even if you are not suffering from a serious illness or pain.

Chapter 4: The Mind-Changing Magic of Meditation

Have you ever wanted to try meditation, but were convinced you would never be any good at it? Meditation is not a competition. It is simply the act of silencing the mind so that you can feel a sense of peace and be in the present. Meditation can be done by anyone, anytime, and anywhere.

This chapter will break down the process of meditation into simple, manageable steps and have you feeling inspired to make it a part of your life.

People often approach meditation with preconceived notions that stand in the way of them getting the most out of the experience. They have specific goals for the outcome of their meditation session: relieving stress, improving memory and focus, etc. While meditation may ultimately help with these things and many more, by treating meditation sessions as a goal rather than simply an intention, we are inadvertently putting undue pressure on ourselves. This can take us out of the moment and set us up for self-judgment, experiencing a sense of disappointment if our goals are not met.

If we could just set the intention of meditating in order to be present, we take away the pressure and judgment and can simply meditate for its own sake. We can decide to practice and see how it turns out. When we are able to relax, we can truly start to quiet our minds and be present in the moment and create a more enjoyable and productive experience.

How to Meditate?
There are many different techniques for meditation. The best part is that there is no one right or wrong way to do it. There is no one-size-fits-all method. It doesn't matter whether it is yoga, saying a mantra,

chanting, counting your breaths, or any of countless other methods. As long as it works for you, it is absolutely right.

Start by setting aside ten to fifteen minutes where you can go into a quiet room without distractions. If you find that this is too much time for you initially, you could start with a smaller amount of time and gradually increase it, or you could set a timer to help you stick with it.

First, let's talk about our breathing and posture. Place a pillow on the floor and sit on it as you cross your legs like a pretzel. If this is a difficult position for you, just do the best that you can while still sitting in a comfortable position. Close your eyes. Breathe in. Breathe out. Soften your jaw. Relax your shoulders. Let all your tension and worries wash away. No one is judging you here. Make sure your back is straight but relax your abdomen and let your belly stick out. Decide if having your eyes open or closed feels best to you. Put your hands on your knees or in your lap.

Now that you are physically ready to meditate, let's work on getting mentally prepared. This may prove to be the harder part. Breathe in through your nose and try to fill up your chest with air while your stomach pushes out a bit. Slowly exhale and count your breaths each time as you repeat the process over and over. Quiet your mind. Do the same steps that we used during our mindfulness practice.

Guided meditation could be an easier way to start getting into meditation. The calm voice of the meditation guide will help you to learn to focus your attention. Another way that you can tune out the noise and concentrate your thoughts is by repeating a mantra or phrase.

You can reach an altered state of consciousness through meditation and relaxation techniques. Focusing your attention and becoming more aware of your physical and mental processes, you can ignore the distractions of your environment. Meditation reduces stress, anxiety, and has other physical and mental health benefits. It leads to increased alpha, delta, and theta brainwaves, which are connected to relaxed states of mind.[xxiii][xxiv]

During the day the brain releases electrical signals which mix to create a unique mental "fingerprint" that we know as a "brainwave pattern." Through these brainwaves, experts can measure your entire human existence; your mood, thoughts, emotions– like anxiety or anger.

"Beta" brainwaves, for example, are responsible to trace your anxious, fearful thoughts. These brainwaves operate on a 13 – 40 Hz left-right wavelength. If you are often anxious, your "beta" brainwaves will be enforced, stronger.

Practicing meditation does quite the opposite; strengthens the "good" brainwaves that are responsible for a happy and healthy state of mind. These are the Alpha, Theta, and Delta brainwaves. You can naturally decrease your anxiety.

Alpha brainwaves work on 7 – 13 Hz. If it's active, Alpha brainwaves help you calm your mind, enhance your creativity, deepen relaxation, increase happiness, and much more.

The Theta Brainwaves on 4 – 7 Hz boost your emotional intelligence. They grant you access to your deepest thoughts, increase inspiration, improve intuition, make you feel more open and connected to the world.

Delta Brainwaves from 0 to 4 Hz enhance your awareness. But besides that they help to slow your aging process, help you have a relaxing sleep, tap into your deepest level of consciousness, and enhance your general wellbeing.[xxv]

As you can see, by tapping into these powerful states of consciousness, meditation's Alpha, Theta, & Delta brainwaves open up a whole world of benefits far beyond having nerves of steel.

There have been many studies conducted to research the positive results people can get from meditation.

A notable study was recently published in the journal *Psychological Science,* which sought to find brain functions that are improved by meditating. The study, led by Katherine MacLean from the University of California—Davis and authored by thirteen additional researchers, found that people who participate in intensive meditation are able to focus their attention and maintain it even during tasks which are considered very boring. The study participants who meditated regularly showed a greater focus, concentration, and attention to detail than their counterparts who did not meditate. The study also found that as people meditated more and improved in their meditation skills, these areas showed an even greater improvement over time. [xxvi]

Other studies have also identified many benefits to meditation beyond improved focus and concentration. People who meditate have often been found to exhibit improved physical health. Meditation has been shown to help improve cardiovascular and immune health, aid in weight loss, help to curb addictions, lower cholesterol, increase energy levels, slow signs of aging, improve circulation, reduce stress, and help to relieve pain for many people. Meditation is a gift we can give ourselves, and it contributes to an overall feeling of wellness by encouraging a healthy lifestyle.[xxvii]

Meditation Activities for Adults

Living in the world of technology and social interconnectedness can increase our stress levels and make it challenging to mentally relax. Meditation offers many options for mental disconnection. Use these activities to stay in the present, calm your anxious brain, and improve your overall wellbeing

The OM practice

The word 'OM' is an ancient mystical syllable, a sacred sound or mantra in Hinduism and Tibetan Buddhism. It has long been used as a tool for meditation purposes. It is usually chanted at the beginning and the end of yoga sessions, but one can use it to aid other meditation practices, as well. [xxviii]

OM is a vibrating sound. If you never heard someone loudly meditating using the OM syllable, here is a video to give you some ideas of how you should "pronounce" it: https://www.youtube.com/watch?v=vH11undyI2o. You can find other OM-meditation videos on YouTube from ten minutes length up to more than three hours. If you are new to OM-meditation, start with a five to ten minutes practice and, when you become comfortable, gradually increase the length of your session.

How to practice OM meditation?

Get yourself in a position that you find comfortable. Dim the lights in your room and, if you can, reduce all noise around you. Start your meditation practice by ringing a bell. After the bell has rung, chant the word 'OM' as you heard in the video. You may feel awkward at first when you do it–especially if your spouse is cleaning potatoes in the kitchen next to you. Fear not, gently notice your feeling of embarrassment. Talk to it, "hi, embarrassed self, I see you, I feel you, and now I let you go." If the feeling didn't diminish, mentally repeat these words over and over again, "I see you, I feel you, I let you go." When you feel more relaxed, return to chanting 'OM.'

Repeat the process of bell ringing followed by the 'OM' chanting at periodic intervals throughout your practice. Each time you recite 'OM' try holding the resonance of the m sound for longer. Close the meditation practice with one bell sound.

Progressive Muscle Relaxation Meditation

Tension often invades our muscles. A rushed day, hard physical labor, increased amount of stress can all result in muscular tightness. This meditation practice will help you to reduce muscle tension.

How to practice Progressive Muscle Relaxation

Meditation?

Begin by lying on your back with your eyes closed. Let your arms and legs naturally fall apart. Keep them stretched out. Take a few deep breaths to calm your mind and tune in to the present moment. Take the time you need to properly relax.

When you are in the here and now, curl your toes tightly and count until thirty or forty-five, depending on how bad you feel by the curled position. Make sure not to cause cramps in your toes. When the thirty seconds have elapsed, relax your toes and focus on the liberating feeling of the release. Welcome the soothing freedom of the relaxed muscles. There is no tension left in them.

Repeat the process of tightening and relaxing the muscle for thirty to forty-five seconds on the remaining body parts. Flex and then release your calves, thighs, buttocks, abdomen, lower and upper back, arms, fingers, neck, and face. Whenever you release a given muscle group from tension, breathe in the freedom, breathe in the lack of tension. Enjoy how your entire being becomes more relaxed, more heavy in the moment.

Gratitude Meditation

Negative thinking can invade mental and physical well-being over time. Gratitude Meditation helps you reduce negative thoughts by focusing on the things you are grateful for.

How to practice Gratitude Meditation?
Go to a quiet place where nobody will disturb you for ten minutes. Dim the lights, use some soothing background sound or music. Sit down comfortably on a chair or pillow. Straighten your back. Imagine that an invisible string is attached to your skull and keeps you in a straight position. Relax your face, neck, and shoulders. Gently breathe in and out.

When your mind becomes more still, think of something in your life for which you are grateful. Then gently whisper out loud "I am grateful for…" and say the name of the object or subject of your gratitude. Let the feeling of gratitude wash over you; that light, heartwarming, dizzy sensation of pure joy. Immerse yourself in this feeling. Gratitude practice is not so much about naming things we are grateful for, but more about recalling how these things or people made us feel. Gratitude is a deep feeling of unlimited satisfaction.

To deepen your gratitude experience, try saving one or two minutes each evening, and recalling five things that you felt very grateful for the given day. This can be anything from a good meal, to some comforting words. When you have the object, recall how it made you feel. Notice how those good feelings wash over your body once more in the form of gratitude.

Imagery Meditation

This type of meditation relies on your imagination. I call it postcard meditation because it feels like being in a beautiful postcard from a faraway land. The goal of this meditation practice is to imagine a beautiful place where you have been, or wish to go, play some gentle meditation music or nature sounds and, for a few minutes, emerge in the imagery experience.

How to practice Imagery Meditation?
Go to a quiet place where nobody will disturb you for ten minutes. Sit comfortably on a chair or pillow. Straighten your back. Imagine that an invisible string is attached to your skull and keeps you in a straight position. Take a few deep breaths. Follow the air as you inhale and exhale. Notice the split-second pauses as your inbreath transforms into outbreath.

When you're relaxed, recall a beautiful scenery–a forest, a seaside, a cozy wooden cottage, whatever pleases your senses the most. Breathe in, intensify the image, breathe out wonder and gratitude. How does this place make you feel? Are there any little twitches or itches in your body? What do you feel? After you update your present moment awareness, try to imagine the natural sounds, smells, textures, views, and tastes in your imagined environment. Gently calm your mind as you think about this wondrous place.

Optional Tools for Meditation

Before you meditate you can feel free to boost the mood of your surroundings. Use scented candles, aromatherapy items, gentle fabrics, soothing music to deepen the meditation experience. Use fragrance of natural essential oils to impact mood. Some essential oils have been used to produce relaxation for a long time. The theory is that just by smelling the fragrance the brain relaxes. Lavender essential oil has been used to induce relaxation and deepen sleep. Rose oil has been used for centuries in perfumes to channel feelings of calmness and serenity.

Ultimately, meditation helps you to slow down and enjoy a fuller life during the session and after. Sometimes I catch myself thinking of all the time that passed by in what seems like the blink of an eye. It is in those moments that I was not being truly present. Those are the times when I was watching my kids' sporting event or activity and thinking of all of the things I had to get done the next day at work. The times when cooking dinner was more of my focus than the little ones asking me to play a game or read them a story. When I was trying to juggle too much instead of being present and missed out on precious moments and memories I can't get back.

Then there are those beautiful memories of family time, which I can replay in my mind with brilliant, vivid detail. They might have happened long ago, but I can relive them like they were just yesterday down to every last minute. The sights, sounds, and even smells are embedded in my mind. Those are the times when I was focused and attentive only to what was happening in the present; when I silenced any other distractions from my mind and truly lived in the moment. The times that I cherish and have enjoyed the most in my life.

I now know that I do not have to wait and wish for a slower-paced life; I can choose to create it for myself. I can choose to live in the present. The best thing of all is that everyone can. Meditation does not require one perfect technique or a set of special skills. Meditation can be done by anyone, anytime, anywhere.

Chapter 5: Acceptance and Commitment Therapy

Acceptance and Commitment Therapy/Training (ACT) is often used in a workplace or psychotherapy setting. ACT takes the principles of mindfulness and mixes it with techniques designed to bring about a change in behavior or increased motivation. The goal of Acceptance and Commitment Therapy/Training is to help us to accept the things that happen which are beyond our control and to deal with the negative thoughts, emotions, and memories which often creep into our minds. By practicing ACT, we become better equipped to deal with physical pain and feelings of failure while feeling less afraid of taking risks and facing uncertainty. ACT encourages us to become more active participants in our own lives and teaches us coping mechanisms for tolerating stress, allowing them us focus on the things in our lives that we can change and have power over.

ACT uses a simple three-step process, which can be easily remembered by the A-C-T acronym:
Step 1: Acceptance,
Step 2: Choosing a direction,
Step 3: Taking action.

Practicing this three-step technique can help you distance yourself from that part of you that is feeling negatively. Not being so involved with your thoughts, you'll better notice, accept, and even embrace the side of you going through pain. By distancing yourself you'll get a rather objective perspective.[xxix]

I will take a closer look at each step to give you a clearer picture how to practice ACT.

Step 1: Acceptance
You may wake up in a bad mood. You might experience anger, anxiety, or sorrow during the day

for no apparent or good reason. What can you do now that the negative thoughts and emotions have invaded your consciousness?

You can engage with them, sink deeper and deeper in the negative emotion and ruin your day.

Or you can try to fight, repress your negative emotions. Fighting an emotion hardly ever works. You'll just end up getting angrier because you're angry and it won't go away. Or you'd get sadder because you can't convince your sadness to go away. Your emotions become a snake which eats its own tail, circling in a vicious loop.

The third option, what ACT promotes, is accepting your emotion for what it is. Allow it to exist, feel it, and experience it. Don't label it just gently notice it. Think "I see you, anger, there you are," or, "I notice I feel anger." Accept this temporary state of mind. Then ask yourself, "is this the way I would prefer to feel in the next few hours or days?" This question brings us to Step 2.

Step 2: Choose a Valued Direction

In a highly emotional, negative state of mind you may think nothing matters. I bet you know that feeling when you are so desperately sad, or so overwhelmingly offended that you think nothing has, or will have, any value until the cause of the negative emotion is not rectified.

In Step 1 you noticed and accepted your negative emotions. Now it's time to look at your core values, desires, and needs. What matters to you? What ideas, principles, people, and objects do you care about the most?

Break through those negative feelings that cloud your judgment, and with all your might focus on something valuable to you. It can be your cat. "I just want to pet my cat." It can be coffee. "Now I just need a cup of coffee!" It can be the wish to hear your mother's voice. "Now I'll just call my mom!"

Deal with your negative emotion. Find a substitute

reason—value that is more important and meaningful. Then…

Step 3: Take Action

By the time you get to this point, you have a clear idea of your wishes—cat, coffee, Mom—so it's time to take action. Pet your cat, go and make a cup of coffee, fetch the phone. It helps if you visualize the action you're about to take. You can even repeat in your head. "Now I will get Fluffy's toy and encourage him into the living room. I can see he is looking for this toy. Then I will lift him and stroke his back." The mind can pay attention on one thought-thread at one time. The point of mentally visualizing the action you are about to take is to refocus your thoughts—far away from the negatives.

This is a rather simplified, home-remedy version of the ACT steps. However, it can work to detach from small, everyday issues. If you have chronic anger problems, or other deeper psychological problems, I'd recommend practicing ACT with a psychotherapist who can guide you through a more advanced version of this technique.

The bottom line of ACT still is:
1. Accept your emotions, memories, thoughts, or other disturbing events that you experience. Allow them to be real.
2. Find and commit to a different direction that brings you to something you value.
3. Take action, making the valued direction a reality.

What you do during an ACT practice is reverse the negative spiral that you got entangled in. Instead of allowing negative emotions to drag you into a downward direction, you deliberately change the direction of your thoughts, and focus on personally meaningful things that get you on an upward spiral.

ACT and Mindfulness

Very much like mindfulness, ACT encourages people to be focused on living in the present, to face it head-on, and to tune out other things that may serve as distractions. It stresses that our feelings are a snapshot of where we were in a given moment in time, and we are capable of experiencing them and then releasing them and moving forward. We are not forever tied to our feelings and they do not define us, just as we should not attempt to cling too tightly to our goals to the point where we may be hard on ourselves if we don't achieve them.

ACT uses mindfulness and other exercises to help us be aware of our thoughts and feelings. It stresses for us to recognize that our thoughts and feelings are just a glimpse into how we are experiencing life at a given moment in time, sort of a snapshot, which can reveal important information to us, but does not need to be held onto and fixated on. Our thoughts and feelings do not need to define us. We are still capable of making our own choices of our own free will. We are able to choose how much focus and weight we give to a certain thought or feeling, and we are able to decide if we want to just let it go and move past it.

The first step to reverse a negative cycle is to identify the destructive behaviors and thoughts that create the cycle.

There is always a trigger that brings the negative emotion or thought to your mind. What is this trigger? How and when does the negative emotion arise? For example, if you have been cheated on before and discovered that your partner kept in touch with their lover on the phone, you may start feeling anxiety every time you see your partner–the old one or a new one–texting on their phone.

The negative emotion elicits a behavior. Pay attention to what behavior takes place when the emotion kicks in. When you start getting anxious seeing your partner texting you may become more irritable, or you might ask, "who are you talking to?" The anxiety pairs with other negative emotions like jealousy, fear of loss, and anger and so the downward spiral gets worse.

Acting on our negative emotion causes some kind of satisfaction in us. In the heat of the moment we might feel good about our behavior triggered by the emotion. Following the example above, questioning our partner may feel the right thing to do because we've been burned once, and we want to make sure it never happens again. This kind of reasoning reinforces the cycle. The feeling of relief, or decreased pressure, may feel like a reward.

However, acting on negative emotions seldom comes without bad consequences. Either we end up hurting someone we love (our new partner might not feel good about our mistrust) or we strengthen a bad habit that is not good for our health.

The answer is mindful acceptance instead of mindless reaction.

When you acknowledge that your negative emotions arise as a consequence of an event, that they elicit a bad behavior, and that they have a reinforcing function, you can then start to make changes in the cycle. Accept that the behavior exists, that it is real. Be kind to yourself, accept that the behavior is understandable, also that it is having negative consequences. Detach from your thoughts and feelings to fully accept your behavior. Don't ignore the part of you that is feeling the negative emotions but create space for yourself to think objectively. Use the mindfulness techniques learned in the previous chapter to calm your mind and bring yourself to the present.

When you feel that you are in the here-and-now, choose a valued direction. Mindfulness meditation can help you to find the best direction in this moment. Do a quick body scanning practice or breathing exercise where you listen to your deepest need. Slowing down, synchronizing your body and mind can give you the best answers for what you should focus and take action on.

Doing what matters. Gain clarity about your core values. Once you have your answers, take action.

Your mind should be calmer now, you successfully detached your true self from your emotions and thoughts. You set your clear goals in accordance with your values. Time to ask yourself, "what's the first step I should do to achieve this goal?"

As we learned earlier in this chapter, acceptance is a crucial ingredient in our spiritual growth. ACT encourages us to accept our current life situation for what it is and be willing to experience it, even if it is not the place we would have liked to be in if we were given a choice.

Acceptance and Commitment Therapy/Training helps those of us who have often lost our center and guiding light because we have become distracted and focused on other difficulties in our lives. It acts as a reset button, attempting to get us to reconnect with our own core values and get back on track with the people and things that mean the most to us and act as our personal guiding principles. This correlates with the notion of setting appropriate goals for ourselves which are more concerned with internal attitudes than external sources of happiness like wealth.

The final guiding principle of Acceptance and Commitment Therapy/Training involves being committed to take action but not having specific expectations for how things will turn out in the end because it recognizes that there are many influences beyond a person's control at work.[xxx]

Chapter 6: Wu Wei - The Do-Nothing Principle

This chapter will present a different way of viewing the world called *wu wei*, offered by Lao Tzu, a revered ancient Chinese writer and philosopher who became the father of Taoism. This philosophy encourages simple and honest living in harmony with nature. Because its focus on harmony and the good way to live, Taoism is often mentioned simply as *the Way*. Unfortunately, there is very little historical evidence to prove when and how was Taoism created, much of the information and beliefs of Taoism are scattered and varying. There are many definitions to the main Taoism terms–wu wei included. With this in mind, I'll try to present this concept using the most widely accepted definitions for it.

The first principle of Taoism states that everything in nature is part of the same whole. We humans are nature; linked to it, created by it, buried in it through the cycle of an ever-unchanging cosmic power.[xxxi] The first principle includes another concept that I'm sure you have encountered in some form in your life, the yin and yang classification. The intertwined black and white shapes, each having a dot of the opposite color in them, symbolize the idea that opposites are needed in order for harmony to exist. We need balance. If you observe the symbol of yin and yang closer, you'll see that each part is equal. There is not more black than white, and not more white than black. This means both are equally important and necessary.

Day and night, sunshine and rain, activity and rest... they are equally important. Everything done in excess thus overthrows the delicate balance. Think about how you feel when you pull an all-nighter to finish some work. You feel like a chocolate mousse left in the sun. You didn't keep your work and body needs in balance. This thought brings us to the–perhaps most important–concept of Taoism called wu wei.

What Does Wu Wei Mean?

Wu wei is often translated as the art of non-doing, the idea that one shouldn't overstretch the natural balance. All actions should come naturally in the worldview of wu wei. We should take life as it comes to us, doing what is necessary in the moment. "When I'm hungry, I eat. When I'm thirsty, I drink. When I feel like saying something, I say it," said Madonna Ciccone, and it fits well into the concept of wu wei.

Let me give you a hypothetical example of wu wei that I don't recommend you follow. Imagine that you grab a vase and throw it at someone. As you are throwing the vase, mentally imagine the reaction of the other person. They can have one of the following responses; either change direction and avoid the vase, block the vase by pushing or kicking it away while it approaches, or they could be hit by it while loudly yelling.[xxxii]

Whatever their reaction is, it will be something spontaneous. A flying vase out of the blue doesn't leave too much room for contemplation. Their natural reaction is a great example of what wu wei means. They acted as life happened to them. However, if the attacked person grabs another vase and throws it at you, they will not practice the concept of wu wei anymore. They turned defense into offense, led by negative emotions and consciously chosen actions. They leave the present moment and act to gain future gratification by taking revenge. That's not wu wei anymore.

In our society, which worships getting things done and staying busy, wu wei seems to go against everything we have been taught is important. Wu wei does not promote laziness or sitting back and waiting for life to happen to us or watching life pass us by. It is a paradigm shift that teaches us to "work smarter, not harder." Non-doing is not literally doing nothing;

it is removing our own self-imposed desires and attempts to control every situation, and, instead, opening ourselves to going with the flow instead of fighting against it.[xxxiii]

When our human nature kicks in and tries to take control, we can become nervous, frustrated, stressed, and impatient if things don't go the way we think they should. Then we enter a cycle where we overdo things. We try too hard and often end up doing more but achieving less than we could if we let go of our preconceived notions of how things should be and accept things for how they are. Instead of wasting our time and energy worrying about what the future outcome will be, we can follow the natural order of things and do our best every moment, hoping that "the now's" best actions will lead to a positive outcome.

By practicing wu wei, we let things happen naturally, taking their normal course. For example, we can't rush learning a skill, we can't rush losing more weight than is natural, we can't work more than physically possible for one day without negative consequences. Whenever we disrespect the balance of our human nature is when problems arise; an illness gets us, our anxiety and stress levels go through the roof.

Lao Tzu said, "If you are depressed, you live in the past. If you are anxious, you live in the future. But if you are at peace, you are in the present." Practicing wu wei can take the stress, worry, and feelings of disappointment out of our bodies and simply let us exist in harmony with ourselves.

Pairing the concept of wu wei with the Acceptance and Commitment Therapy steps from the previous chapter can produce magical results. Accept that you can't do more than your energy and time permits, choose to do what you need each moment to the best of your knowledge as your valuable commitment, and then take action–do what each moment requires.

This doesn't mean that you shouldn't do work-related things. Quite the contrary, there are very specific periods in your life when that's exactly what you should do to your best ability in the present moment. Do work when it is time to do work. Nothing else. Do work to exercise your best working self in the moment. Believe that by doing so, the future will be rewarding. This way you'll be more productive, efficient, and effective in the use of your time and energy. Accomplish more while trying less. You'll spend less effort and energy because you won't be distracted. You may feel less anxious, be able to sleep better without the mental chatter in your head talking about all the things you have to get done in the future.

How to practice wu wei?
If you have already begun your meditation journey, you are already on your way to practicing wu wei. Meditation involves quieting the mind and letting it be unoccupied by other thoughts and distractions as you live in the moment and are aware of what is

happening within and around you.

Wu wei takes the principle of mindfulness meditation a step farther.

First, take the opportunity to spend time in nature. Don't just pass through it. Stop and take the time to really experience it. Quietly observe it. Be still and become connected to it. This will be your first step in being able to go with the natural flow of life instead of imposing your own will and fighting against it.[xxxiv]

Try doing a ten- to twenty-minute meditation session of your choice. Tune in your body deeply. Usually, mindfulness meditation encourages non-reactivity, but this time do something different. Pay attention to every sensation in your body and respond to them when they occur. In nature it is not hard to notice different external stimuli affecting your body. Respond to these stimuli with wu wei. When grass tickles your feet, scratch it. When a bug hums around your face, shoo it. When wind caresses your face, be grateful for it. In the moment–right when it happens. Notice your spontaneous reactions to your distractions. There is no right or wrong reaction. Just go with the flow of the events and focus on staying present.

Take a lesson from nature. Go against the grain of human belief, which assumes that scarcity is the norm. We often are hesitant to give and share with others based on the fear that if we do, we may not have enough for ourselves. Nature acts in the opposite way, being very giving and generous. The sun gives us all of its light and heat without running out or becoming depleted. From seeds grow fruit. The fruit is food to many living creatures, and the fruit also produces many seeds which allows many more animals to be fed in the future. In times of hurricanes, the gopher tortoise opens its burrow home to other species as a refuge, including some animals which may typically be a threat to them. A burrow may serve as a home or refuge to up to four hundred other species. They are all able to peacefully coexist and share a living space without fear of harm. By practicing to be more generous we bring ourselves closer to the natural flow of things and become more connected to nature. We may even find that through giving, we come to receive more than we could ever have thought possible.

The next step toward joining the natural flow of the universe is to let go of our fixed notions of what our lives should look like. We sometimes become so fixated on our expectations of how things should be that we close ourselves off to new possibilities. If we can let go of these preconceived ideas, we can open ourselves up to accepting things as they really are and welcome what life gives us every passing moment.

Wu wei believes that natural flow occurs spontaneously. Being open and spontaneous helps us live life with less stress and headache. A farmer can do everything humanly possible to prepare for a good harvest–till the soil, fertilize and irrigate, carefully plant seeds for optimum performance and growth, and protect against pests and disease–but he or she can't predict and guarantee the outcome with any certainty. He did the most he could. Now it's time for him to be hopeful and harvest the fruits of his hard work. If he did the best he could, he will harvest the best outcome that could have happened amidst the unpredictability of nature–which is out of his control. There are limits to what we can do on our own. We just have to let go of control and work hard to do our best every moment, be open to spontaneously accept opportunities, and relaxed that we did our best.

Chapter 7: Energy Management With Mindfulness

When do you feel that you are under the most stress? If you are like the average person, it is probably when you feel like you are running out of time and can't stay on schedule to finish what you started. What do you usually do when you come to this realization? I bet you start browsing websites and books that offer you tips and techniques for successful time management. However, they may be leading you down a less productive path. Research now suggests that it is more important for us to focus on managing our energy rather than struggling to manage time which often proves elusive and, since it comes in a finite amount, is nearly impossible to truly manage.[xxxv]

In our fast-paced lives it is natural to think that if we push ourselves harder we should be able to accomplish more, but it is impossible to be productive if we try to keep high energy levels throughout our entire day. We simply can't function at a maximum energy level one hundred percent of the time. We need to work smarter, not harder.

When we allow ourselves to get stressed out because we feel like our time is running out, our ability to think clearly, and be mindful, decreases greatly. Through mindfulness, we can change our stress levels and productivity. If we focus on the things we can control, like keeping our energy levels in balance, we will start to see an improvement in all aspects of our daily lives.

Energy balance is the delicate relationship between the energy you take in and the energy you consume. When you use the same amount of energy as you intake, your energy level will be balanced. This comes with additional benefits like your body weight staying the same, better mood, and focus.[xxxvi]

There are two negative sides in energy management. One side of the energy imbalance is when one consumes more energy than one burns. This may often be the case based on reports about the rapidly growing obesity epidemic in the U.S. and other countries.[xxxvii] These people are taking in more fats, carbohydrates, and proteins, than they are burning. The reason behind this trend may be the high accessibility to food twenty-four hours per day. Convenience stores, fast-food chains, snack machines are all offering an abundance of calorie-rich foods for those "in need."

The other end of the energy imbalance spectrum is when someone consumes less nutrients than his or her body needs to successfully complete every activity. These people often lose weight to an unhealthy level. They feel constant stress and fatigue, keeping themselves "alive" with a high dosage of caffeine. This kind of lifestyle can lead to a lot of health problems like high blood pressure and hypertension.[xxxviii]

The Biology of Energy Management

Most of your body's total energy usage per day goes to the so-called basal metabolism. This is the minimum amount of energy your body needs to keep up bodily functions while you're resting; for example how much energy your burn while breathing, keeping your blood circulating, maintaining cellular activities and so on. In other words, basal metabolism is your basic energy consumption.

The basal metabolic rate (BMR) shows the rate at which energy is used for each of these functions. Physical activities, like eating your salami sandwich or digesting it, are not included in the BMR.

The basal metabolic rate differs in the case of each person. The influencing factors of one's BMR are size and body composition among others. People who have a bigger frame usually have a higher BMR because the bigger surface releases more heat which pushes up the BMR. Body composition means the proportion of fat and fat-free mass. Lean muscles are more active than fat, thus they need more energy. Consequently, the more lean muscle you have, the higher your BMR will be and vice versa. Men usually have more lean muscle than women, thus they generally have a higher BMR. Age also influences the basal metabolic rate as aging reduces lean muscle mass in one's body thus the elderly have a lower BMR. [xxxix]

Hormonal levels also can have an influence on one's basal metabolic rate. An underactive thyroid gland (also called hypothyroidism) produces insufficient hormones, thyroxine (T4) among others. This hormone affects the metabolic rate. Thus its underproduction can lead to fatigue, a sense of slowness. [xl]

Last but not least, let's mention calorie intake as a BMR influencing factor. Whenever one starts a diet one can notice how the change in nutrition affects metabolism. The simplified equation looks like this, if you lower your calorie intake you lower your BMR. This is a frustrating catch 22 situation because your goal with the low calorie intake is to lose weight. However, because you eat less calories, also your ability to burn calories goes down.[xli]

What happens with the rest of your energy intake which is not used for your BMR? Some of it gets burned by doing physical activities. I don't mean going to the gym or for a run but also things like washing the dishes, bringing the report to your boss, washing the car, reading a book, even meditating. All these activities create thermogenesis (which could be literally translated to heat creating). Energy burning generates heat. The body also uses energy when it is processing the food you eat. Digestion, nutrient absorption all require energy. Did you ever feel like heat is running through your body after you consumed a substantial dinner? It was because of the "thermic" effect–the heat generated by burning energy on consuming the food.

Considering all these aspects of energy consumption, what do you think? Are you in energy balance? Do you consume more than your body burns overall? Or do you consume less? These are very important questions that require an immediate answer if you wish to improve your everyday life quality, concentration, focus, and productivity. Meditation can help you calm your mind to an extent. But a growling stomach can easily throw you off the Zen bridge.

Having a strong mind-body connection is very important. Mindfulness meditation can't fill your stomach by itself, but it can help you raise awareness of your state of hunger, thirst, or fatigue. Practicing the mindful eating technique presented in the previous chapters can help you become more aware of your actual state of hunger. You can try to do the same exercise with thirst. Check your body and ask yourself how thirsty you are four-five times a day;

just for a few seconds. If you find that you're thirsty, drink some water.

What about fatigue? This is a trickier question. Sometimes, even when we are in energy balance from a nutritional point of view, we may still experience sluggishness or decreased focus. The Federal Aviation Administration conducted a study which found that taking short breaks during long working sessions caused a sixteen percent improvement in focus and awareness.[xlii]

Why is this? Taking breaks is actually following your body's natural rhythm. Nathaniel Kleitman, a physiologist and sleep researcher who co-discovered REM sleep, is famous for finding that we alternate between light and deep sleep in ninety minute time periods.[xliii] Kleitman also went on to find that our bodies follow the same ninety minute rhythm during the day as we move between periods of being more and less alert. [xliv]

According to Tony Schwartz, in his article in the Harvard Business Review, after people work very intensely for longer than ninety minutes, they begin to rely on stress hormones as their source of energy. He writes that the prefrontal cortex of the brain starts to shut down and people begin to struggle to think clearly.

Too often, people try to counteract these natural periods of low alertness by consuming caffeine or sugary foods. It is well known that any energy boost one receives from consuming these foods or drinks is short lived, so people may be better served by following their bodies' natural rhythm and taking short breaks to rest and regroup.[xlv]

Research on ultradian rhythms conducted by Peretz Lavie agrees with these findings. When people work productively for ninety minutes and then take a short fifteen-twenty minute break, they are acting more in sync with their bodies' natural energy cycles and are able to stay focused and maintain higher energy levels throughout the day.[xlvi]

This cycle is being followed by people in all different professional fields. Some of the most talented violinists in the world share the common schedule of practicing their instrument intensely for ninety minutes and then taking a fifteen-minute break. The U.S. Army Research Institute also conducted a study finding that people have better focus and increased levels of energy for a longer time when they work for ninety minutes and then take a fifteen-twenty minute break.[xlvii]

Dr. Alejandro Lleras, a psychology professor at the University of Illinois, believes it is crucial for people to build in occasional breaks from work, regardless of how they decide to spend their few minutes of rest. A study was conducted on eighty-four subjects who were expected to perform a simple task on the computer for an hour. The people who were allowed to take two short breaks during that time had a consistent performance through the whole hour, while the people who weren't given a break had a decrease in performance over time. After our bodies and minds are exposed to stimulation constantly for an extended period of time, our brains begin to view the stimulus as being unimportant and our minds erase it from our awareness. Taking a break is imperative in order for our brain to view the stimulus as being new enough to allow us to focus on it again.[xlviii]

A big part of being mindful means living in the present moment and being connected to our bodies. The better we are able to know ourselves and our bodies and how they are linked, the more productive we will be able to be in our daily lives. Most people have times of the day when they usually feel more mentally sharp and focused and have more physical energy. If we are able to plan our schedules around those peak performance periods, we may find that our days can become much more productive.

While not everyone's body has the exact same BMR,

Circadian Rhythms of high and low function, there are often similar times of day for many people. It is common for many to find it hardest to concentrate and stay focused between the hours of twelve-four p.m. Studies have found that the brain is typically best at dealing with difficult cognitive tasks after ten a.m., once the body has been fed and the brain has had a chance to become fully awake.[xlix]

Try to focus your intense energy level periods on the most difficult things you need to do in the late morning and then build in a break in the afternoon during the times of most distraction. Creative thinking has been shown to increase during the afternoon hours for many people. When you're tired in the late afternoon hours, it's a great time to be creative because you're not filtering everything as much as when you're alert and overly critical. Boredom is also an indicator that you're not doing anything satisfactory at the moment and allows your mind to wander toward new, creative ideas. Give yourself some time to think about problems which may require some creativity to solve during that time period may prove to be productive.[1]

While it would be nice if we could make the stress in our lives disappear, unfortunately it is simply not possible to erase it. We can, however, create focused lives for ourselves and choose to concentrate on the things we can control, like where and when to best spend our energy. By listening to our bodies and minds, we will find infinite ways to work smarter, not harder, and reclaim some of the productivity we may have lost.

Energy Management Exercises

Energizing Yoga Breathing
When we talk about mindfulness and meditation we can't really separate them from yoga. I call yoga the mindfulness meditation in motion. The first exercise I wish to present to you is a very simple, yet effective and energizing breathing technique. You can practice it any time, anywhere, in your suit or in pajamas.

Stand up and place your feet shoulder width apart. Inhale slowly and deeply. While you inhale, lift your arms straight above your head and even lean back a little bit if you find it comfortable. As you exhale, bring your arms down and lean forward trying to touch your shins or toes. Then again, as you breathe in, slowly stand up straight, lift your arms, straighten your back. With the exhalation, try touching your toes. Don't rush the breathing. Optimally count to eight as you inhale and again to eight as you exhale. Repeat this motion at least ten times and see how you feel.

This asana improves your blood circulation and wakes up your entire body. Whenever you feel tired and in need of a break, try to practice it for a few minutes and allow the magic to happen.

Double the break you think you need
Wish to take a five minute break? Make it ten. An hour break? Make it two. When you feel you're at the limit of your energy but at the same time you feel

anxious about the amount of things you need to do, it's when you disrupt your body-mind connection. You wish to use more mind at the expense of your body. You probably underestimate the toll your hard work is taking on your body and mind. Be kind to yourself, double your rest time, meditate to calm your brain and reset it. You will see that you'll be much more productive after the break and you will get more things done in less time.

Take care of your body.
Mens sana in corpore sano, healthy mind in a healthy body. This means eating nutritious food, drinking enough water, getting good sleep, exercising several times a week, and going to health checkups regularly. If your body is prepared for the challenges of the day your mind will perform better, too. This is the type of advice where you raise your brows and think 'duh' but are you actually, really doing these things? The 'duh' advices are the simplest to understand yet the hardest to follow. We're always looking for some kind of complicated, über-scientific solution when

the best, and most effective methods are right in front of us. Here's my challenge for you. Stop looking for the best high-end advice and for a week follow this simple plan:

- sleep eight hours,
- eat fresh vegetables and fruits every day, have nutritious lean meat in one of your daily meals (beef, chicken, fish, seafood),
- drink at least sixty-eight oz. (two liters) of clean, unflavored water every day,
- walk or jog for twenty minutes.

If your life quality doesn't improve after a week of following these simple steps, and you still feel fatigued and tired, maybe you should talk to your family doctor and go to a health checkup. Sometimes there are more complex health reasons for sluggishness than lack of sleep. Don't Google medicate yourself, go to a doctor and find out the cause of your decreased activity.

Avoid being "busy."

Being busy is a clear sign of poor time management and the opposite of good energy management. Before you commit to do something, make sure that it is high priority, it adds value to your life in some way, and you have time to do it. The following questions could help narrow down your commitments:

- What will happen if I say yes? What happens if I say no?
- Is this a top-priority engagement?
- How does it align with my values?
- Will this engagement enrich my life?
- How does my body and mind feel about this commitment?
- What do I need right now?

Take a moment to think before you say yes to the requests you get or the plans you make. Ask and answer the questions above to see how a certain engagement fits into your life. Sure, you can't be too picky with work-related tasks. Fulfilling your job is why you get your salary even if the task itself doesn't enrich your life in any particular way. If certain assignments make you feel terrible and overly exhausted, you can try to talk about it with your boss and make some adjustments (get more time to finish it, or some creative freedom).

Chapter 8: Mindfulness in Relationships and Work

Mindfulness in Relationships

Can being mindful really help improve our relationships? Research supports this idea. In the February 2016 issue of the *Journal of Human Sciences and Extension,* a meta-analysis found that mindfulness is connected to greater relationship quality. The study combined results from twelve studies and found that mindfulness has a reliable impact on relationship satisfaction.[li]

Mindfulness can make people more empathetic and compassionate toward others, as well as less impulsive. It improves one's ability to respond to conflict more calmly and constructively and not get overwhelmed by anger.

The scientific reason for this is hidden in the amygdala. The two little almond-shaped group of nuclei process memories, decision-making and emotional responses including fear, anxiety, and aggression as their primary role.[lii]

Mindfulness makes the amygdala of the brain less reactive. It improves the connection between the amygdala and the prefrontal cortex, which better equips people to calm themselves when they feel angry or afraid. This can make people less likely to perceive the behavior of their partner as a threat to their well-being and happiness and feel less of a need to protect themselves. They become more willing to protect their relationship instead.

Mindfulness strengthens another area of the brain as well. The anterior cingulate cortex (ACC) is responsible for our self-perception and regulating our attention, impulses, and emotions. It is the part of the brain that also allows our thinking to be flexible enough so we can see things from perspectives other than our own. It gives us the ability to change instead of staying fixated on one negative view of our partner or ourselves.[liii]

The ACC helps us to break away from past traumas and insecurities we may have that can negatively impact our relationships. Mindfulness can help us to calm ourselves, so we aren't tempted to engage in behaviors like avoiding intimacy or controlling our partners. In essence, it makes us better equipped to grow and change in our relationships and within ourselves as we are faced with new obstacles throughout our lives.[liv]

Finally, mindfulness helps to change our insula for the better. The insula is the part of our brain connected to our attention control, emotional regulation, and interoception. We become more aware of our own feelings as well as our partner's, allowing us to be more compassionate. Mindfulness allows us to be more accepting of our partners instead of being obsessed with what we perceive to be their flaws. We start to see them in a more positive light. We begin to understand that their behavior is related to their life experiences and are more likely to be understanding and forgiving. Being more aware of our feelings makes us less likely to overreact to stressful triggers and allow them to negatively impact our relationships.[lv]

Researchers from the University of San Diego, Georgetown University, the University of California and others conducted a joint study to see if mindfulness techniques help military personnel respond better to an aversive stimulus.

Soldiers face a higher risk for cognitive, emotional, and physiological compromise as they are exposed to stressful environments for a long period of time. The research investigated whether mindfulness practice modifies neural processing of interoceptive distress in infantry marines who were just about to start their pre-deployment training and be later deployed to Afghanistan.

The soldiers were separated into two groups. The control group received the regular training. The second group received additional twenty-hour mindfulness-based fitness training. Both groups were exposed to inspiratory breathing loads as part of the training. Those who underwent the mindfulness-based fitness training showed a significant mitigation of right anterior insula and anterior cingulate cortex during the experience of loaded breathing. The results of the research enforce the hypothesis that mindfulness training "changes brain activation such that individuals process more effectively an aversive interoceptive stimulus." [lvi]

By allowing us to be more present and attentive to our partners, we are better able to be intimate and loving and have happier and more connected relationships. We are less likely to argue over every little thing and become emotionally uncontrollable. We can recognize when we are starting to behave in unhealthy ways and change our responses before things get out of hand.

How to improve our relationships by practicing mindfulness?

Deep Listening

When our mind is full of anxious thoughts about the future we tend to not listen carefully to our loved ones, and people who talk to us in general. Other times we are more preoccupied with what to respond to them than to deeply analyze what is written between the lines. Our mind is busy, agitated, we want to sound smart and offer a solution. But usually people would rather be heard than hear a superficial, smart-but-not-relevant solution that lacks true empathy. When we are overly focused on ourselves rather than the other, we miss much of what people are telling us.

This is the main reason why we have such difficulty remembering someone's name when we first introduce ourselves. The problem isn't with our memory, but with the fact that we don't pay attention to someone when he says his name. We are too preoccupied saying our names correctly.

Just like we realize instantly when someone isn't truly listening to us, our conversation partner will know right away when we are not listening, as well. Deep listening shows people that we are genuinely interested in them, we value their honesty and time, we show respect, caring, and appreciation. All these things make or break the quality of a relationship–be it romantic or professional.

How to practice deep listening?
When you engage in a conversation, look into people's eyes when they're speaking to you. Make a conscious effort to pay attention on what they are saying. Resist the temptation to let your focus decrease. When you feel that your mind is drifting away, gently stop the person who is talking and recapitulate what you've heard so far. You can say something like "sorry to interrupt you, I just want to

make sure I understand you correctly. When you say that… do you mean this…" Fill in the gaps with the topic of the conversation. This technique allows you to make sure you indeed understood your conversation partner and gives him or her a positive feedback about your sincere interest. I know that it is tempting to offer an instant solution to others' problems but before you respond with, "what I think you should do" type of answers, make sure that your conversation partner is looking for solutions from you instead of just wishing to be heard.

Mindful Speaking

Most human conflicts root in simple miscommunication. Because of poor listening–discussed in the exercise above–people might misunderstand each other's intentions. When we have a casual conversation we often speak aloud our first thoughts. Rarely do we pause before speaking, thinking about how our words might be interpreted by others. We jump to the conclusion that just because we understand what we want to say, the other person will have the same level of understanding, too. While there is no absolute guarantee that if we stop and mindfully think our message through, the other person will not misunderstand us, the probability of a miscommunication can be highly reduced.

How to practice mindful speaking?

When you engage in a conversation, practice a ten-second mindfulness breathing technique to bring yourself to the present moment. Then after listening deeply to your partner, consciously, with complete awareness, count to three before giving a gut answer. These three seconds are enough to assess if what you're about to say is offensive or prone to create a misunderstanding. If you identify that you shouldn't say what you're about to say, just tell your partner, "let me think for a second about my answer." Then take the time you just won to choose your words more carefully. Think about what your goal with this conversation is: to be right above all costs or to have a constructive and compassionate conversation with your partner. If the latter, choose loving, compassionate, and respectful words, with a calm and encouraging tone. You can mention that you disagree with your partner's opinion, however, assure them that you accept that they see things as they do. Tell them that you are willing to listen more about their side and in exchange you'd like to tell them your side to find a compromise.

Mindfulness at Work

Our workplace is often filled with stress and competitiveness as we strive for promotions and raises. This can be a slippery slope if we are not equipped to deal with stress without simply reverting to our brain's autopilot responses, or if we do not shift our thinking to creating better and healthier goals for ourselves. Through our examination of mindfulness so far, we have learned that judging others and ourselves is a detriment that takes away our energy and focus from more important matters. This is no exception in the workplace. We need to acknowledge that we are making these judgments and put them aside so that we can direct our attention to more productive grounds.

Drew Hansen has found that a growing number of well-known and successful companies are recognizing the benefits of incorporating mindfulness principles into their workplace culture. Apple, Google, McKinsey & Company, Deutsche Bank, Procter & Gamble, Astra Zeneca, General Mills, and Aetna have all implemented mindfulness programs for their employees. Many are already noticing pretty astounding results.

According to the Forbes article, General Mills reports that after a seven-week mindfulness training seminar, "eighty-three percent of participants said they were taking time each day to optimize personal productivity—up from twenty-three percent before the course. Eighty-two per cent said they now make time to eliminate tasks with limited productivity value—up from thirty-two percent before the course. And among senior executives who took the course, eighty percent reported a positive change in their ability to make better decisions, while eighty-nine percent said they became better listeners."[lvii]

Hansen goes on to find that the leaders of Silicon Valley are firm supporters of mindfulness meditation and how it can help them to better lead their companies. They have identified meditation practices that they incorporate into their daily business lives:

1. "Anchor your day with a contemplative morning practice (e.g., Breathe, Zen, Kabbala, etc.).

2. Before entering the workplace, remind yourself of your organization's purpose and recommit to your vocation as a leader.

3. Throughout the day, pause to be fully present in the moment before undertaking the next critical task.

4. Review the day's events at the close of the day to prevent work stresses from spilling into your home life.

5. Before going to bed, engage in some spiritual reading."[lviii]

Even successful businesses are now seeing the benefits that mindfulness training and meditation have to offer their employees. Increasing the emotional awareness of employees creates a more positive workplace environment and leads to greater productivity.

Now the question becomes how we incorporate mindfulness principles into our workplace on a daily basis. Here are a few easy suggestions that anyone can begin to implement immediately.

How to practice mindfulness at your workplace?

The first way we can improve our workplace environment is by shifting our way of thinking. Instead of expecting the worst in our weekly meetings (which usually proves to be unhelpful), we can wish the meeting's leader the best. Send out a positive thought that they will have a productive and beneficial meeting. Or just acknowledge that attending meetings is part of your job, it's part of the team leader's job, too. Even if he knows he has nothing noteworthy to share, he has to hold the meeting and might hate it even more than you do. Try to be compassionate. Not only will you have a more positive attitude, you may become a better listener, or a more active and helpful participant in the meeting.

Another tip for implementing mindfulness in your workplace is simply to look people in the eye when you are speaking with them. In other words, practice deep listening discussed in the relationship section. Your colleagues will see that you value what they have to say.

Taking a minute for meditation to take ten deep breaths before you begin a new task can reset the connection between your body and mind, readjust your focus on the new problem you need to solve and gives your mind a moment of rest.

Perhaps one of the most powerful ways we can improve our workplace environment for our colleagues and ourselves is just by smiling. You will find that your smile can instantly decrease everyone's stress levels and cause improved moods, making for a more enjoyable day at work for everyone involved.

Final Words

Mindfulness is more than a habit. It is a way of life in which we make a conscious effort to quiet our thoughts, calm our minds, and live in the present moment–where life actually happens.

Practicing mindfulness not only helps us obtain a better life quality, but also provides many benefits, from improving our brain function and immune system to strengthening our relationships and allowing us the opportunity to stop being so hard on ourselves.

Mindfulness is impactful in all areas of our lives. It is my sincere hope that you will have read something in this book that will encourage you to look within yourself and find your own motivation to begin your journey to practicing mindfulness. I wish you good luck and great success as you embark on a truly rewarding new way of life.

Reference

Ackerman, Courtney. MBSR: 25 Mindfulness-Based Stress Reduction Exercises and Courses. Positive Psychology Program. 2017. https://positivepsychologyprogram.com/mindfulness-based-stress-reduction-mbsr/

Albertson, Ellen R., Neff, Kristin D., Dill-Shackleford, Karen E. Self-Compassion and Body Dissatisfaction in Women: A Randomized Controlled Trial of a Brief Meditation Intervention. Springer link. Original paper: Mindfulness, Volume 6, Issue 3, pp. 444–454. 2015. https://link.springer.com/article/10.1007/s12671-014-0277-3#page-1

American Psychological Association. Delaying Gratification. American Psychological Association.

https://www.apa.org/helpcenter/willpower-gratification.pdf

Atkinson Pain Research Laboratory, Division of Neurosurgery, Barrow Neurological Institute. Interoception: the sense of the physiological condition of the body. Pub Med. 2003. https://www.ncbi.nlm.nih.gov/pubmed/12965300

Barnes, S., et al. (2007). The role of mindfulness in romantic relationship satisfaction and response to relationship stress. Journal of Marital and Family Therapy, 33(4), 482-500.

Center for Anxiety and Traumatic Stress Disorders. Randomized controlled trial of mindfulness meditation for generalized anxiety disorder: effects on anxiety and stress reactivity. Pub Med. 2013. https://www.ncbi.nlm.nih.gov/pubmed/23541163

Clayton. Five Senses Mindfulness Exercise. Clayton. 2018.

https://www.clayton.edu/Portals/541/docs/Five%20Senses%20Mindfulness%20Exercise.pdf

Colier, Nancy. LCSW. Why Our Thoughts Are Not Real. Psychology Today. 2013. https://www.psychologytoday.com/blog/inviting-monkey-tea/201308/why-our-thoughts-are-not-real

Davidson, R., et al. (2003). Alterations in Brain and Immune Function Produced by Mindfulness Meditation. Psychosomatic Medicine, 65, 564-570.

Fischer, D., Messner, M., & Pollatos, O. Improvement of Interoceptive Processes after an 8-Week Body Scan Intervention. Frontiers in Human Neuroscience, 11, 452. 2017. http://doi.org/10.3389/fnhum.2017.00452.

Flook, L., Smalley, S.L., Kitil, M.J., Dang, J., Cho, J., Kaiser-Greenland, S., Locke, J. & Kasari, C. (2008, April). A mindful awareness practice improves executive function in preschool children.

Forbes, Bo. Interoception: Mindfulness in the Body. LA Yoga. 2015. https://layoga.com/practice/yoga/interoception-mindfulness-in-the-body/

Greenberg, Melanie. PhD. Five Ways Living Mindfully Can Help You Reach Your Goals. Psychology Today. 2013. https://www.psychologytoday.com/blog/the-mindful-self-express/201305/five-ways-living-mindfully-can-help-you-reach-your-goals

Greenberg, Melanie. PhD. Can Mindfulness Make Your Relationship Happier? Psychology Today. 2016. https://www.psychologytoday.com/blog/the-mindful-self-express/201606/can-mindfulness-make-your-relationship-happier

Hansen, Drew. A Guide To Mindfulness At Work. Forbes. 2012. https://www.forbes.com/sites/drewhansen/2012/10/31/a-guide-to-mindfulness-at-work/#6d94217825d2

Johnson, Susan K. David, Zhanna., Goolkashian, Paula. Mindfulness Meditation Improves Cognition. 2010. DOI: 10.1016/j.concog.2010.03.014 · Source: PubMed. 2010.
https://www.hs-neu-ulm.de/fileadmin/user_upload/Über_uns/Familie_und_Soziales/BIZEPS/Mindfullness_meditation_improves_cognition.pdf

Johnson. 44 Self Discipline Strategies, Backed By Science. 1 Percent Braver. 2016. http://1percentbraver.com/self-discipline/

Katherine A. MacLean, Emilio Ferrer, Stephen R. Aichele, David A. Bridwell, Anthony P. Zanesco, Tonya L. Jacobs, Brandon G. King, Erika L. Rosenberg, Baljinder K. Sahdra, Phillip R. Shaver, B. Alan Wallace, George R. Mangun, Clifford D. Saron. Intensive Meditation Training Improves Perceptual Discrimination and Sustained Attention. Sage Journals. 2010.

http://journals.sagepub.com/doi/abs/10.1177/0956797610371339

Lazar, S., et al. (2005). Meditation experience is associated with increased cortical thickness. NeuroReport, 16(17), 1893-1897.

Lueke, Adam. Gibson, Brian. Mindfulness Meditation Reduces Implicit Age and Race Bias The Role of Reduced Automaticity of Responding. Sage Journals. 2014. http://journals.sagepub.com/doi/abs/10.1177/1948550614559651

Manson, Mark. Why I'm Wrong About Everything (And So Are You). Mark Manson. 2013. https://markmanson.net/wrong-about-everything

McGonigall, Kelly. PhD. The Problem with Progress: Why Succeeding at Your Goals Can Sabotage Your Willpower. Psychology Today. 2011. https://www.psychologytoday.com/blog/the-science-willpower/201112/the-problem-progress-why-succeeding-your-goals-can-sabotage-your

McGreevey, Sue. 'Turn down the volume.' Harvard Gazette. 2011. http://news.harvard.edu/gazette/story/2011/04/turn-down-the-volume/

Medicine Net. Medical Definition of Proprioception. Medicine Net. 2018. https://www.medicinenet.com/script/main/art.asp?articlekey=6393

Napoli, M., Krech, P., & Holley, L. (2005). Mindfulness Training for Elementary School Students: The Attention Academy. Journal of Applied School Psychology, 21(1), 99-125.

Omidi, Abdollah. Zargar Fatemeh. Effects of mindfulness-based stress reduction on perceived stress and psychological health in patients with tension headache. NCBI. J Res Med Sci. 2015 Nov;

20(11): 1058–1063. doi: 10.4103/1735-1995.172816. 2011. https://www.ncbi.nlm.nih.gov/pmc/articles/PMC4755092/

Pickert K (February 2014). "The art of being mindful. Finding peace in a stressed-out, digitally dependent culture may just be a matter of thinking differently". Time. 183 (4): 40–6.

Ravenscraft, Eric. Make Friends With Your Future Self to Get Better at Future Planning. Lifehacker. 2015. http://lifehacker.com/make-friends-with-your-future-self-to-get-better-at-fut-1750265016

Richards, Chip. Wu Wei: The Ancient Art of Non-Doing. Uplift. 2016. http://upliftconnect.com/wu-wei-ancient-art-non-doing/

Singh, N., et al. (2006). Mindful Parenting Decreases Aggression, Noncompliance, and Self-Injury in Children with Autism. Journal of Emotional and

Behavioral Disorders, 14(3), 169-177.

Staff, Mindful. What is Mindfulness? Mindful. 2014. https://www.mindful.org/what-is-mindfulness/

Teo, Soon. DO NOTHING if you want to be your best. Tao in you. 2016. http://tao-in-you.com/do-nothing-is-doing-something/

Quintiliani, Anthony. PhD. What is Interoception and Why is it Important? Mindful Happiness. 2017. http://mindfulhappiness.org/2017/what-is-interoception-and-why-is-it-important/

Endnotes

---

[i] Staff, Mindful. What is Mindfulness? Mindful. 2014. https://www.mindful.org/what-is-mindfulness/

[ii] Lazar, S., et al. (2005). Meditation experience is associated with increased cortical thickness. NeuroReport, 16(17), 1893-1897.

[iii] Davidson, R., et al. (2003). Alterations in Brain and Immune Function Produced by Mindfulness Meditation. Psychosomatic Medicine, 65, 564-570.

[iv] Tang, Y., et al. (2007). Short-term meditation training improves attention and self-regulation. PNAS, 104(43), 17152-17156.

[v] Barnes, S., et al. (2007). The role of mindfulness in romantic relationship satisfaction and response to relationship stress. Journal of Marital and Family Therapy, 33(4), 482-500.

[vi] Singh, N., et al. (2006). Mindful Parenting Decreases Aggression, Noncompliance, and Self-Injury in Children with Autism. Journal of

Emotional and Behavioral Disorders, 14(3), 169-177.

[vii] Napoli, M., Krech, P., & Holley, L. (2005). Mindfulness Training for Elementary School Students: The Attention Academy. Journal of Applied School Psychology, 21(1), 99-125.

[viii] Flook, L., Smalley, S.L., Kitil, M.J., Dang, J., Cho, J., Kaiser-Greenland, S., Locke, J. & Kasari, C. (2008, April). A mindful awareness practice improves executive function in preschool children.

[ix] Center for Anxiety and Traumatic Stress Disorders. Randomized controlled trial of mindfulness meditation for generalized anxiety disorder: effects on anxiety and stress reactivity. Pub Med. 2013.
https://www.ncbi.nlm.nih.gov/pubmed/23541163

[x] Lueke, Adam. Gibson, Brian. Mindfulness Meditation Reduces Implicit Age and Race Bias The Role of Reduced Automaticity of Responding. Sage Journals. 2014.
http://journals.sagepub.com/doi/abs/10.1177/1948550614559651

[xi] Albertson, Ellen R., Neff, Kristin D., Dill-Shackleford, Karen E. Self-Compassion and Body Dissatisfaction in Women: A Randomized Controlled Trial of a Brief Meditation Intervention.

Springer link. Original paper: Mindfulness, Volume 6, Issue 3, pp. 444–454. 2015.
https://link.springer.com/article/10.1007/s12671-014-0277-3#page-1

[xii] Johnson, Susan K. David, Zhanna., Goolkashian, Paula. Mindfulness Meditation Improves Cognition. 2010. DOI: 10.1016/j.concog.2010.03.014 · Source: PubMed. 2010.
https://www.hs-neu-ulm.de/fileadmin/user_upload/Über_uns/Familie_und_Soziales/BIZEPS/Mindfullness_meditation_improves_cognition.pdf

[xiii] Quintiliani, Anthony. PhD. What is Interoception and Why is it Important? Mindful Happiness. 2017.
http://mindfulhappiness.org/2017/what-is-interoception-and-why-is-it-important/

[xiv] Forbes, Bo. Interoception: Mindfulness in the Body. LA Yoga. 2015.
https://layoga.com/practice/yoga/interoception-mindfulness-in-the-body/

[xv] Fischer, D., Messner, M., & Pollatos, O. Improvement of Interoceptive Processes after an 8-Week Body Scan Intervention. Frontiers in Human Neuroscience, 11, 452. 2017.
http://doi.org/10.3389/fnhum.2017.00452.

[xvi] Medicine Net. Medical Definition of Proprioception. Medicine Net. 2018.
https://www.medicinenet.com/script/main/art.asp?articlekey=6393

[xvii] Clayton. Five Senses Mindfulness Exercise. Clayton. 2018.
https://www.clayton.edu/Portals/541/docs/Five%20Senses%20Mindfulness%20Exercise.pdf

[xviii] Pickert K (February 2014). "The art of being mindful. Finding peace in a stressed-out, digitally dependent culture may just be a matter of thinking differently". Time. 183 (4): 40–6.

[xix] Mental Health Foundation. Mindfulness Report. Mental Health Foundation. 2010.
https://www.mentalhealth.org.uk/sites/default/files/Mindfulness_report_2010.pdf

[xx] Omidi, Abdollah. Zargar Fatemeh. Effects of mindfulness-based stress reduction on perceived stress and psychological health in patients with tension headache. NCBI. J Res Med Sci. 2015 Nov; 20(11): 1058–1063. doi: 10.4103/1735-1995.172816. 2011.
https://www.ncbi.nlm.nih.gov/pmc/articles/PMC4755092/

[xxi] Ackerman, Courtney. MBSR: 25 Mindfulness-Based Stress Reduction Exercises and Courses. Positive Psychology Program. 2017. https://positivepsychologyprogram.com/mindfulness-based-stress-reduction-mbsr/

[xxii] Ackerman, Courtney. MBSR: 25 Mindfulness-Based Stress Reduction Exercises and Courses. Positive Psychology Program. 2017. https://positivepsychologyprogram.com/mindfulness-based-stress-reduction-mbsr/

[xxiii] EOC Institute. How Meditation Cancels Out Anxious Brainwaves. EOC Institute. 2018. https://eocinstitute.org/meditation/alpha-theta-delta-brainwaves-how-meditation-relieves-anxiety/

[xxiv] Haliwell, Ed. Meditate With Intention, Not Goals. Mindful. 2015. https://www.mindful.org/meditate-with-intention-not-goals/

[xxv] EOC Institute. How Meditation Cancels Out Anxious Brainwaves. EOC Institute. 2018. https://eocinstitute.org/meditation/alpha-theta-delta-brainwaves-how-meditation-relieves-anxiety/

[xxvi] Katherine A. MacLean, Emilio Ferrer, Stephen R. Aichele, David A. Bridwell, Anthony P. Zanesco,

Tonya L. Jacobs, Brandon G. King, Erika L. Rosenberg, Baljinder K. Sahdra, Phillip R. Shaver, B. Alan Wallace, George R. Mangun, Clifford D. Saron. Intensive Meditation Training Improves Perceptual Discrimination and Sustained Attention. Sage Journals. 2010. http://journals.sagepub.com/doi/abs/10.1177/0956797610371339

[xxvii] Harvard's Men Health Watch. Exercising to Relax. Harvard Health Publishing. 2018. https://www.health.harvard.edu/staying-healthy/exercising-to-relax

[xxviii] Zelaya, Rachel. What's The Meaning of OM? Gaia. 2017. https://www.gaia.com/article/what-meaning-om

[xxix] S. C. Hayes, J. B. Luoma, F. W. Bond, Akihiko Masuda, J. Lillis Acceptance and Commitment Therapy: Model, processes and outcomes. Georgia State University Scholar Works. 2006. https://scholarworks.gsu.edu/cgi/viewcontent.cgi?article=1085&context=psych_facpub

[xxx] Greenberg, Melanie. PhD. Five Ways Living Mindfully Can Help You Reach Your Goals. Psychology Today. 2013. https://www.psychologytoday.com/blog/the-mindful-self-express/201305/five-ways-living-mindfully-can-help-you-reach-your-goals

[xxxi] Personal Tao. Taoism 101: Introduction to the Tao. Personal Tao. 2018. https://personaltao.com/taoism/taoism-101/

[xxxii] Whittemore, Jessica. Taoism as "The Way": Yin and Yang & the Wu-wei Concept. Study.com. 2018. https://study.com/academy/lesson/taosim-as-the-way-yin-and-yang-the-wu-wei-concept.html

[xxxiii] Teo, Soon. DO NOTHING if you want to be your best. Tao in you. 2016. http://tao-in-you.com/do-nothing-is-doing-something/

[xxxiv] Richards, Chip. Wu Wei: The Ancient Art of Non-Doing. Uplift. 2016. http://upliftconnect.com/wu-wei-ancient-art-non-doing/

[xxxv] Schwarz, Tony. McCarthy, Catherine. Manage Your Energy Not Your Time. Harvard Business Review. 2007. https://hbr.org/2007/10/manage-your-energy-not-your-time

[xxxvi] Buchanan, Leigh. Why Managing Your Energy Is the Key to Maximum Productivity. Inc. 2015. https://www.inc.com/leigh-buchanan/maximize-productivity-manage-energy.html

[xxxvii] Health Data. Obesity and Overweight Increasing Worldwide. Health Data. 2016.

http://www.healthdata.org/infographic/obesity-and-overweight-increasing-worldwide

[xxxviii] Hartley Terry R. PhD, William R. Lovallo PhD, Thomas L. Whitsett MD, Bong Hee Sung PhD, Michael F. Wilson MD. Caffeine and Stress: Implications for Risk, Assessment, and Management of Hypertension. Online Library. 2007.
https://onlinelibrary.wiley.com/doi/full/10.1111/j.1524-6175.2001.00478.x

[xxxix] Black, A.E. Critical evaluation of energy intake using the Goldberg cut-off for energy intake: basal metabolic rate. A practical guide to its calculation, use and limitations. International Journal of Obesity volume 24, pages 1119–1130. 2000.
https://doi.org/10.1038/sj.ijo.0801376

[xl] Alexandra M Johnstone, Sandra D Murison, Jackie S Duncan, Kellie A Rance, John R Speakman; Factors influencing variation in basal metabolic rate include fat-free mass, fat mass, age, and circulating thyroxine but not sex, circulating leptin, or triiodothyronine, The American Journal of Clinical Nutrition, Volume 82, Issue 5, 1 November 2005, Pages 941–948,
https://doi.org/10.1093/ajcn/82.5.941

[xli] Donnelly, Joseph E. Nicolaas P Pronk, Dennis J Jacobsen, Stephanie J Pronk, John M. Effects of a very-low-calorie diet and physical-training regimens on body composition and resting. American Society for Clinical Nutrition. Am J C in Nutr. 1991;54:56-61. 1991.
https://www.bewegenismedicijn.nl/files/downloads/full_text_donnelly_1994_effects_of_diet_and_training.pdf

[xlii] Hampton E. Matthew. Enhanced FAA Oversight Could Reduce Hazards Associated With Increased Use Of Flight Deck Automation. Federal Aviation Administration. 2016.
https://www.oig.dot.gov/sites/default/files/FAA%20Flight%20Decek%20Automation_Final%20Report%5E1-7-16.pdf

[xliii] Reed, Christopher. Nataniel Kleitman. The Guardian. 1999.
https://www.theguardian.com/news/1999/aug/25/guardianobituaries3

[xliv] Kolowich, Lindsay. The Science of Productivity: How to Get More Done in a Day. Hubspot. 2017.
https://blog.hubspot.com/marketing/science-productivity

[xlv] Lavie, Peretz, Zomer, Jacob, Gopher, Daniel. Ultradian Rhythms in Prolonged Human Performance. 32. 1995.

https://www.researchgate.net/publication/235129211_Ultradian_Rhythms_in_Prolonged_Human_Performance

[xlvi] Lavie, Peretz, Zomer, Jacob, Gopher, Daniel. Ultradian Rhythms in Prolonged Human Performance. 32. 1995. https://www.researchgate.net/publication/235129211_Ultradian_Rhythms_in_Prolonged_Human_Performance

[xlvii] Patal, Neil. When, How, and How Often to Take a Break. Inc. 2014. https://www.inc.com/neil-patel/when-how-and-how-often-to-take-a-break.html

[xlviii] Nauert, Rick PhD. Taking Breaks Found to Improve Attention. Psych Central. 2018. https://psychcentral.com/news/2011/02/09/taking-breaks-found-to-improve-attention/23329.html

[xlix] Alhola, Paula, and Päivi Polo-Kantola. "Sleep Deprivation: Impact on Cognitive Performance." Neuropsychiatric Disease and Treatment 3.5. 553–567. 2007. https://www.ncbi.nlm.nih.gov/pmc/articles/PMC2656292/

[l] MacLellan, Lila. Almost everyone is creative around the same time every day. QZ. 2018. https://qz.com/work/1214666/theres-a-best-

time-of-day-to-be-productive-and-do-creative-work/

[li] Greenberg, Melanie. PhD. Can Mindfulness Make Your Relationship Happier? Psychology Today. 2016. https://www.psychologytoday.com/blog/the-mindful-self-express/201606/can-mindfulness-make-your-relationship-happier

[lii] Amunts K, Kedo O, Kindler M, Pieperhoff P, Mohlberg H, Shah NJ, Habel U, Schneider F, Zilles K (December 2005). "Cytoarchitectonic mapping of the human amygdala, hippocampal region and entorhinal cortex: intersubject variability and probability maps". Anatomy and Embryology. 210 (5-6): 343–52. doi:10.1007/s00429-005-0025-5. PMID 16208455.

[liii] Kral Schuyle, Mumford, Rosenkranz, Lutz, Davidson. Impact of short- and long-term mindfulness meditation training on amygdala reactivity to emotional stimuli. NCBI. PMID: 29990584. DOI: 10.1016/j.neuroimage. 2018. https://www.ncbi.nlm.nih.gov/pubmed/29990584

[liv] Maron-Katz A. Ben-Simon E. Gruberger M. Sharon H. Hendler T. ,Cvetkovic. A neuroscientific perspective on meditation. Research Gate. 2018. https://www.researchgate.net/profile/Eti_Ben-

Simon/publication/271173240_A_Neuroscientific_Perspective_on_Meditation/links/5534dad70cf2ea51c1334b64/A-Neuroscientific-Perspective-on-Meditation.pdf

[lv] Haase L, Thom NJ, Shukla A, et al. Mindfulness-based training attenuates insula response to an aversive interoceptive challenge. Social Cognitive and Affective Neuroscience. 2016;11(1):182-190. doi:10.1093/scan/nsu042.

[lvi] Haase L, Thom NJ, Shukla A, et al. Mindfulness-based training attenuates insula response to an aversive interoceptive challenge. Social Cognitive and Affective Neuroscience. 2016;11(1):182-190. doi:10.1093/scan/nsu042.

[lvii] Hansen, Drew. A Guide to Mindfulness at Work. Forbes. 2012.
https://www.forbes.com/sites/drewhansen/2012/10/31/a-guide-to-mindfulness-at-work/#2e36e8fa25d2

[lviii] Hansen, Drew. A Guide to Mindfulness at Work. Forbes. 2012.
https://www.forbes.com/sites/drewhansen/2012/10/31/a-guide-to-mindfulness-at-work/#2e36e8fa25d2